Student Book

Tessa Lochowski and Annie Altamirano

Contents

UNIT 1 — **How can we eat well?**
- Reading 1 — **Factual text:** The Sweet Tooth Truth! — Page 6
- Reading 2 — **Fiction:** When in Rome — Page 12

UNIT 2 — **Why are some buildings famous?**
- Reading 1 — **Factual text:** As High as the Sky — Page 22
- Reading 2 — **Fiction:** From Paris to Peru — Page 28

UNIT 3 — **How can we protect wild animals?**
- Reading 1 — **Factual text:** Once They're Gone, We Can't Bring them Back — Page 38
- Reading 2 — **Fiction:** Where There's No Return — Page 44

UNIT 4 — **What can we do with our trash?**
- Reading 1 — **Fact:** Waste Not, Want Not! — Page 54
- Reading 2 — **Fiction:** Rubbish Revival — Page 60

UNIT 5 — **How can we choose our jobs?**
- Reading 1 — **Factual text:** Biographies — Page 70
- Reading 2 — **Fiction:** Ahoy There! — Page 76

UNIT 6 — **What happens in extreme conditions?**
- Reading 1 — **Factual text:** Extreme Climates! — Page 86
- Reading 2 — **Fiction:** The Medallion Movers — Page 92

UNIT 7 — How and why do fashions change?

| Reading 1 | **Factual text:** The Fashion Museum | Page 102 |
| Reading 2 | **Fiction:** The Treasure in the Attic | Page 108 |

UNIT 8 — How has entertainment developed?

| Reading 1 | **Factual text:** Winning Combinations! | Page 118 |
| Reading 2 | **Fiction:** Movie Stars in the Making | Page 124 |

UNIT 9 — Why are adventure stories popular?

| Reading 1 | **Factual:** Sailing Around the World – Solo! | Page 136 |
| Reading 2 | **Fiction:** Pete and the Pirates | Page 140 |

UNIT 10 — Why do we raise money for charity?

| Reading 1 | **Factual text:** What Is Biblioburro? | Page 150 |
| Reading 2 | **Fiction:** Miremba's Dream Comes True | Page 156 |

UNIT 11 — How are we similar but different?

| Reading 1 | **Fiction:** Anne of Green Gables | Page 166 |
| Reading 2 | **Factual text:** Nature or Nurture? | Page 172 |

UNIT 12 — How did people live in the past?

| Reading 1 | **Factual text:** Railway Revolution! | Page 182 |
| Reading 2 | **Fiction:** William's Lucky Day | Page 188 |

1

How can we eat well?

Listening
- I can understand the main points of an interview.
- I can identify key details in factual talks.

Reading
- I can predict what a text is about.
- I can identify specific information.

Speaking
- I can make suggestions about activities.
- I can talk about personal experiences.

Writing
- I can write short texts on familiar topics.

1 💬 **Look at the picture and discuss.**

1 What can you see in the picture?
2 What's the boy doing?
  Do you think he's healthy?
3 Why does he like eating this food?
4 What do you think he eats in a normal day?

2 **Read and make notes. Then compare your answers with a friend.**

1 What's your favorite food and why do you like it?
2 Is it good for you?
3 Is there anything you can't eat?

3 ▶ 1-1 BBC **Watch the video about food. Why is food important?**
Circle **T** (true) or **F** (false).

1 Food keeps us healthy.   T   F
2 Food gives us energy.   T   F
3 All food is good for us.   T   F
4 Food can affect how we feel.   T   F

5

Pre-reading 1

1 Discuss with a friend. What's a healthy diet?

> **Reading strategy**
>
> Use context and pictures to guess the topic.

2 Read the text, look at the pictures, and answer. Which items can you identify? What do we mean by good fats?

BLOG

Good fats

So, eating fat doesn't make you fat? Yes, that's right. There are good fats and bad fats and we now know which fatty foods are actually good for us!

Let's take a look at olive **oil** and **butter** – they both contain good fats. Olive oil is great to drizzle on a salad, and it's great to spread butter on a slice of bread.

3 🎧 1-02 Read *The Sweet Tooth Truth!* What's a balanced diet?

Reading 1

THE SWEET TOOTH TRUTH!

Eating a balanced and varied diet is important for our health. We should eat different types of food, in the right amounts. So, where does sugar come into this?

1 Lots of us love sugar and we have a sweet tooth, but sugar is in lots of our food and too much isn't good for us. Let's start with breakfast and cereal – it tastes good and is a very popular food all over the world.

2 It's hard to find time for breakfast, and it's easy to think a quick bowl of cereal looks like a sensible and healthy option. It contains **fibre** and **carbohydrates**, and can be a good source of **dairy** and **protein** from the milk. It's sometimes packed with good **vitamins** and **minerals** like **calcium** and **iron** too.

3   The question: "How much sugar do we need?" is an important one. Let's think about sugar cubes* – we're advised to eat no more than around six cubes of sugar each day (for 7 to 10 year-olds), but a small serving of some cereals can contain half our daily intake. Sometimes that's more than three sugar cubes! That's a lot of sugar and lots of us are eating nearly two or three times more sugar than we need!

4   With sugary cereal for breakfast, our levels of sugar go up very high, very quickly. We get a quick boost of energy, but then our energy levels drop quickly too. This can make us sleepy, moody and unhappy. We can also find it difficult to think. This isn't good when we need to study and learn at school! Cereal looks good but we need to be careful.

5   Like good **fats** and bad fats in our diet, we can look at healthy sources of sugar. Sugar is also in **vegetables** and fruit. This type of sugar helps us manage the levels of sugar in our bodies. When we replace a sugary breakfast cereal with plain cereal or yoghurt and a tasty piece of fruit, our sugar levels rise slowly. Our energy will last longer and we probably won't feel hungry again until lunchtime. It's easy to concentrate and we don't feel tired or sleepy.

6   Too much sugar now can mean problems in the future, for example tooth decay, problems with weight, and diseases like diabetes. The good news is we can make small changes now and reduce foods and drinks with added sugar. Try changing fizzy drinks for water or no-added sugar drinks, or ice cream for sugar-free jelly. Can you change your sweet tooth?

*1 CUBE = 4g SUGAR

4   How do you feel after eating different foods? What food do you eat to give you more energy?

Comprehension 1

1 Read *The Sweet Tooth Truth!* again and answer.

1. What happens when we have too much sugar?
2. How can your energy last longer?

2 Check (✓) the sentence that best summarizes the text.

1. We should eat sugar every day. ☐
2. We should eat cereal for every meal. ☐
3. The ideal balance of sugar is a mix of sugar in fruit and sugar in soda. ☐
4. Think about the kind of sugar we eat and manage our sugar levels. ☐

3 Read the article again and match the headings to the paragraphs on pages 6-7. What helped you decide?

a	Full of energy!	1
b	Sugar is everywhere	2
c	A quick breakfast	3
d	A change for the future	4
e	Sugar cubes	5
f	Feeling sleepy!	6

Listening 1

4 A nutritionist knows a lot about food and staying healthy. What do you think a nutritionist does?

Listening strategy
Make predictions before you listen.

5 🎧 1-03 Listen to a nutritionist talking to a group of children. What kinds of food or drink does he ask about?

6 🎧 1-04 Complete the summary. Then listen again and check.

Gabriel helps people ¹ .... well. Fruit contains ² .... and a large orange contains ³ .... sugar cubes! Fruit is good for us because it contains ⁴ .... , ⁵ .... , and fiber. It also has ⁶ .... Fruit has nutritional benefits and is ⁷ .... for us.

7 💬 Discuss with a friend. How much sugar do you eat every day? Is it a lot and what changes can you make to eat less?

Vocabulary 1

1 Look at the words in bold in *Sweet Tooth Truth!*. What do you think they mean?

2 Match the definitions to the words in bold on pages 6–7. Were your ideas correct?

1 These are found in food, for example, iron and calcium. ....
2 The food group that includes milk, cheese, and yogurt. ....
3 It gives us energy and you can find them in bread, pasta, and cereal. ....
4 This is a word for foods like onions, carrots, and potatoes. ....
5 This is good for our teeth and bones and is found in dairy products. ....
6 This helps us keep warm and is in different foods we eat. ....
7 You can find this in meat, milk, and eggs. ....
8 We can spread this on our bread. ....
9 An element found in some foods. ....
10 This helps food move through your body. ....
11 A kind of fat which isn't solid. ....
12 These have letters and numbers in their names. ....

3 Read *The Sweet Tooth Truth!* again. Find examples of food and write them in the chart. Can you add more examples?

Protein	Carbohydrates	Fat	Dairy	Sugar

4 💬 Write a food diary for a day (what you eat for breakfast, lunch, and dinner). Talk about your food diary with a friend.

> Do you eat a lot of … ?   I don't really like …   I like …
> I think I eat …   What about you?   What about (protein)?

Grammar 1

1 Watch Part 1 of the story video. Why doesn't Kim drink tea with honey? Then read and complete.

The pizzas .... !

2 Read the grammar box and match.

Grammar

What are you cooking, Mom? It **smells delicious** and **looks good**.
Wow! Those cakes **look tasty**. Can I try one?
I don't know what this is. It **tastes like** beef, but it **looks like** chicken.

1	These pizzas taste	a	like fish, but I don't know what it is.
2	Fruit cake. Yummy! It smells	b	an orange, but it's very small.
3	This is strange. It tastes	c	very good, Mom. Thank you!
4	What's that? It looks like	d	delicious. Does it contain apples?

3 Read *The Sweet Tooth Truth!* again and circle examples of looks good, looks like, and tastes good.

4 Read and circle.

1 The bread you're cooking **smells / smells like** delicious.
2 Yummy! This curry **tastes / tastes like** great!
3 Is this fish? It **looks / looks like** chicken to me.
4 Those cakes **look / look like** beautiful – they have flowers on them.

10

5 Look and complete the sentences. Use *taste*, *look*, and *smell* and your own ideas. Then compare with a friend.

WHAT IS IT?

Wow! This ¹_____ nice. It ²_____ soup. It ³_____ vanilla ice cream. It's really nice. It isn't my favorite flavor, but it ⁴_____. Look, it has these things, they ⁵_____ leaves. It ⁶_____ fruit, but I'm not sure.

Speaking 1

6 Think of a food and ask your friend to guess the food. Make sure you write down the food you guess.

> **Speaking strategy**
> Use hand gestures to make yourself understood.

James:	Is it meat?	**James:**	Does it look like fruit?
Mark:	No.	**Mark:**	Yes.
James:	Does it taste nice?	**James:**	Is it a tomato?
Mark:	Yes.	**Mark:**	Yes!

7 Use your list. You're planning a menu for tomorrow. How healthy is it? Can you make it healthier?

> Pasta with tomato is healthy.

> We can make it healthier if we add salad.

Pre-reading 2

1 Discuss with a friend.

1 When do you need the most energy?
2 What's the most important meal of the day for you? Why?

> 📖 **Reading strategy**
>
> Check your understanding while reading.

2 💡 Read. Why do you think Eneida eats pancakes for breakfast?

I need a lot of energy at the start of the day! I do a lot of sports and I realize that I need to eat well to be healthy, so it's important for me to have a nutritious breakfast. It has to be filling and tasty, too. Sometimes I have **pancakes** with fruit and strawberry **jelly**. I also like cereal with milk, fruit, and nuts. But my breakfast isn't always sweet. Let's have a closer look at the things I eat.

3 🎧 1-05 Read *When in Rome*. Why did Harry's parents wake him up?

Reading 2

WHEN IN ROME

Harry was suddenly awake. It was still dark outside, but Harry was happy it was Saturday and the weekend was here. Something was different and a bit strange … again.

Harry couldn't quite see the clock at the end of his bed. He got up to investigate and looked at the time … 5 a.m.! It's too early! Harry went back to bed, but he could hear Mom and Dad. They're walking upstairs, thought Harry. "Wake up, Harry! It's breakfast time."

"What, no, it can't be, it's Saturday. It's 5 a.m. I'm sleeping!"

"Not today, you aren't. We're taking you on a journey. Put this on and come downstairs."

Harry was sleepy, but he put the clothes on and looked in the mirror. "What's this?" he thought. It looks really old!

"Mom, Dad, these clothes are … Wait, why are we all wearing these old clothes?"

"We're in ancient Rome today, Harry!" said his mom. "In ancient Rome, everyone got out of bed before the sun came up and … here's your breakfast." Harry looked down to see a **bread roll** and a cup of water. "Oh, um, thank you." Harry wasn't excited about breakfast today. He preferred peanut butter and jelly on toast.

Harry's parents gave Harry a different breakfast every Saturday morning. Sometimes breakfast was from a different country and sometimes it was from a different time in the past. Harry ate a **noodle** and **beef** soup from Vietnam last Saturday. His favorite was **omelet**, **grilled** fish, and **miso soup** from Japan.

"Harry, don't worry. This is the last time – we had a lot of of ideas, but we can't think of any more!" said Harry's dad. "'But we want you to think about breakfast for tomorrow … a brain breakfast!"

"Yes I'll think about it in bed!" said Harry. He was very happy and thought this was a great idea! He learned all about brain foods last week at school and how brain foods can help our memory and concentration. He started to think … oily fish, so **salmon**! … **boiled** or **fried** eggs, nuts, **broccoli**, seeds, tomatoes, avocados, …. oooh and a lot of chocolate … these are all healthy brain foods, but what can we eat for breakfast with of all of these?

Harry got up early on Sunday and prepared breakfast for everyone.

"Mom, Dad! Breakfast's ready!"

4  Do you think diets are better now or in the past? Why? What do you think Harry made for breakfast?

Comprehension 2

1 Read *When in Rome* again. Where was Harry's breakfast from this morning?

1 Vietnam   2 Ancient Rome   3 Japan

2 Read again and answer.

1 Do you think Harry usually likes breakfast?
....

2 Why do Harry's parents want him to make breakfast?
....

3 Does Harry want to make a brain breakfast?
....

4 What does brain food do?
....

3 Use examples from the story to complete the chart.

BREAKFAST FROM THE PAST:	Bread and water, Ancient Rome ....
BREAKFAST FROM DIFFERENT COUNTRIES:	....
BREAKFAST WITH SOUP:	....
BRAIN FOODS:	....

Listening 2

Listening strategy
Listen for specific words and information.

4 Listen to the conversation. What are they talking about? Check (✓) the things you hear.

dinner ☐   soda ☐
milk ☐   bananas ☐
apples ☐   reading ☐
sleep ☐

5 Listen again. Circle **T** (True) or **F** (False).

1 She says bananas can help us sleep well.   T   F

2 Bananas can help our body relax.   T   F

3 Jessica says we should drink soda before bed.   T   F

6 Discuss with a friend. Do you eat or drink before bed? Do you think food can make a difference to how you sleep?

Vocabulary 2

1 Find these words in *When in Rome*. Which are sweet foods? Which describe how something is cooked?

> beef   boiled   bread roll   broccoli
> fried   grilled   jelly   miso soup
> noodles   omelet   pancakes   salmon

2 Read *When in Rome* again and complete the quiz.

1 We can eat them for breakfast with fruit. They're ....
2 They look like spaghetti and are sometimes used in soups. They're ....
3 Something you can spread on your bread. It's ....
4 Cooking eggs like this makes them hard. It's ....
5 This is when food is cooked in very hot oil. It's ....
6 A kind of green vegetable. It's ....

3  Six words from Activity 1 are missing from the quiz. Write down these words. Work with a friend and write quiz questions for these words. Ask another pair your questions.

4 Read *When in Rome* again and think. Then ask and answer the questions with a friend.

1 Which breakfast from around the world would you like to try? Is it healthy?
2 What would you make for breakfast for Harry's parents?

I would like to try …

I would like to make …

Grammar 2

1   Watch Part 2 of the story video. Where are they? Then complete.

I'_____ _____ in the _____ _____ .

2   Watch Part 3 of the story video and answer. What happened to the robots? What do you think the doctor is going to do with the honey?

3 Look at the grammar box and read.

> **Grammar**
>
> You can use *will* to talk about quick decisions that you make:
> **I'll look** in the Indian restaurant.
> **I'll eat** more fruit.
> I **won't drink** soda every day.

4 Read *When in Rome* again and circle examples of *will*.

5 Read and and complete the sentences with the correct form of the verbs in parentheses.

1 We _____ (go) to the Chinese Restaurant.
2 I _____ (look) for my book now.
3 I _____ (have) any cake.
4 I _____ (eat) more fruit and vegetables.

16

6 Read the dialog. Complete with 'll eat, and won't eat.

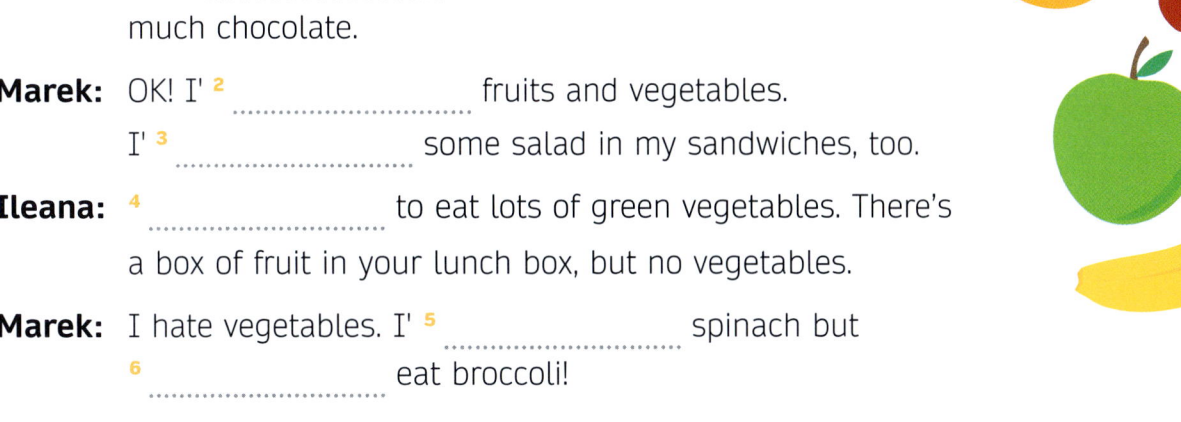

Ileana: There's too much chocolate in your lunch box. You ¹_____ stay healthy if you eat too much chocolate.

Marek: OK! I' ²_____ fruits and vegetables. I' ³_____ some salad in my sandwiches, too.

Ileana: ⁴_____ to eat lots of green vegetables. There's a box of fruit in your lunch box, but no vegetables.

Marek: I hate vegetables. I' ⁵_____ spinach but ⁶_____ eat broccoli!

7 Think about the things you eat and drink. What unhealthy things do you eat or drink? What changes could you make so you're healthier? Complete the chart.

What **kind of food do you like**?
I like chocolate.
Is it good/bad for you?
No, it isn't./Yes, it is.

	unhealthy	healthy
1	I drink a lot of soda.	I'll drink more water.
2		
3		
4		

Speaking 2

8 Use your answers from Activity 7. Ask and answer with a friend.

What kind of food do you like?

I like fruit.

Is that good for you?

Yes, it is.

Writing

1 Scan the text. Answer the questions.

1 What does Josef like to eat?
2 What food groups does Josef eat?

2 Read the text. Check your answers from Activity 1.

JOSEF'S TIPS

Healthy food – healthy mood!

To feel happy, have energy, and be healthy, we should do these things:

TIP 1: Eat a balanced diet. We shouldn't eat a lot of the wrong food because we can feel sleepy, grumpy, and find it difficult to concentrate at school.

TIP 2: Find a favorite meal that's balanced. My favorite meal is lasagne with salad. It has pasta, vegetables, meat, and cheese. This means it has carbohydrates, protein, and fat.

TIP 3: Think about food groups. We should eat some food from each of the three main food groups (carbohydrates, protein, and fat) every day. A good balance of healthy food means we'll feel great!

3 When we give advice, we use *should* and *shouldn't*. Read the text again and circle *should* and *shouldn't*.

1 What's your favorite meal?
2 What are the ingredients? What makes it healthy or unhealthy for you?
3 How often should you eat it?

4 Find or draw pictures of your healthy eating tips. Then go to the Workbook to do the writing activity.

Writing strategy

We can use **should** and **shouldn't** to give advice, for example:
We **should** eat a balanced diet.
We **shouldn't** eat a lot of sugar.

Now I Know

1  How can we eat well? Look back through Unit 1. Think about why a healthy diet is important. Write down some reasons.

1. A balanced diet has protein, fat, and carbohydrates.
2. Fruits and vegetables give us vitamins and minerals.
3. Drinking and eating well give us energy and help us concentrate.

....

....

2 Choose a project.

Do a survey about eating habits.

1. Decide what information you want to find out from your class.
2. Write some questions you can ask.
3. Ask your questions and write down your findings.
4. Prepare and present the information to the class.

or

Write advice about healthy eating.

1. Find information about healthy foods and unhealthy foods, and how people can make healthy choices.
2. Find or draw pictures that show the most important information.
3. Write notes to explain the pictures.
4. Make a poster for the class.

Read and circle for yourself.

I can understand the main points of an interview. I can identify key details in factual talks.

I can predict what a text is about. I can identify specific information.

I can make suggestions about activities. I can talk about personal experiences.

I can write short texts on familiar topics.

2

Why are some buildings famous?

Listening
- I can recognize a speaker's point.
- I can extract information about past events.

Reading
- I can identify specific information.
- I can make basic inferences.

Speaking
- I can talk about personal experiences.
- I can talk about plans for the near future.

Writing
- I can write descriptive texts about familiar places.

1 💬 Look at the picture and discuss.

1 What type of building can you see?
2 What do you think this building is?
3 What do you think it's like inside?
4 Who designs buildings like this?

2 Read and make notes. Then compare your answers with a friend.

1 Can you think of words to describe this building?
2 Do you like it? Why?/Why not?
3 What materials are used?
4 Why is the building famous?

3   Watch the video. Circle T (true) or F (false).

1 You need to study for a long time to be an architect. T F
2 Architects don't need to understand science. T F
3 Rosie's favorite building is the Gherkin. T F
4 Battersea Power Station is a massive project. T F

21

Pre-reading 1

1 Discuss with a friend.

1 When did you last visit an interesting or famous building?
2 Why is it interesting or famous?

> **Reading strategy**
>
> Scan a text in order to find specific information.

2 Read and answer. What's the name of the building? What kind of building is it?

At the Eden Project in Cornwall, UK, you can see what looks like huge bubbles sitting on the land. These **structures** are called biomes. Inside the biomes are different plants from all over the world. There's a rainforest biome that is tall enough to fit the Tower of London into it! The Eden Project was designed by Grimshaw Architects and the whole project is bigger than 35 football pitches!

3 Read *As High As the Sky*. 1-08 Find two numbers that show you how buildings are taller now than in the past.

Reading 1

As High As the Sky

Today, we can make buildings in almost any shape or size, and quickly too! When we compare the buildings of today to the buildings built many years ago, we can see lots of changes in design. Just compare the famous building known as the Gherkin in London with the Parthenon in Greece!

In the 19th century, people tried new ideas and started to design and build in ways they hadn't before. It was an important time in history when people started to work differently. Instead of hand-made products, things were made in larger numbers in factories. The production of materials changed. For example, the production of iron increased. This was just one change, and there were a lot more changes that resulted in an exciting time for architecture. Buildings and other **constructions**, like **bridges**, could be bigger, longer or taller than before.

We all know the Eiffel **Tower**. This was the work of Gustave Eiffel. He finished the tower in 1889 and at that time, it was the tallest building in the world. It was 324 **metres** high. Today, the Eiffel Tower is still the tallest building in Paris, but since the Eiffel Tower, architects have designed and created much taller buildings around the world.

Gustave also worked on the famous **monument**, the **Statue** of Liberty, in New York, which continues to **attract** tourists with its large number of tall buildings. William Lamb finished the Empire State Building in 1931. It's 381 metres tall and in 1931 it was the tallest building in the world. From the 102nd floor, visitors can see New York City, but is it still the tallest building in the world?

From the 1970s, **architects** designed bigger buildings. Tons of iron, steel, aluminium, **concrete** and glass were used to build the Burj Khalifa in Dubai, in the UAE. How tall is it? It's 828 metres tall and has got 57 elevators! It's three times as tall as the Eiffel Tower and almost twice as tall as the Empire State Building! So, as you can see, some **modern** buildings are bigger and taller – some are **massive**!

4 How are the buildings in the pictures different from or similar to buildings in your country? Is there a famous building or monument in the place where you live?

23

Comprehension 1

1 Look at the numbers below. Scan *As High As the Sky* and find what they refer to.

> 1889   381   828   57

2 Organize the buildings in the chart in order of height and age: *Empire State Building*, *Eiffel Tower*, and *Burj Khalifa*.

Tallest	Oldest
1	1
2	2
3	3 Burj Khalifa
Shortest	Youngest

3 Read *As High As the Sky* again and answer.

1 Why was the 19th century an important time for architecture?
2 Why did structures get bigger, taller, or longer?

Listening 1

4 Listen to Abbie. Does Abbie's city have any famous buildings?

> **Listening strategy**
>
> Ignore words that seem less important.

5 Listen again and circle.

1 Abbie is from **Madrid** / **Bilbao**.
2 There is a famous **building** / **bridge** in Bilbao.
3 The Guggenheim opened in **1997** / **2012**.
4 Frank Ghery is an **engineer** / **architect**.

6 What does an architect do? What skills do you think an architect needs? Do you know any famous architects? Discuss with a friend.

Vocabulary 1

1 Match the words to their definitions.

1 tower
2 monument
3 statue
4 construction
5 architect
6 bridge
7 meters
8 attract
9 modern
10 massive
11 structure
12 concrete

a   This is a structure built in a public place to celebrate an important person or event.
b   This is a tall, thin structure or a building that stands alone.
c   This goes from one side of a place, for example a river, to the other.
d   A person or animal made of stone, wood, metal, or another material.
e   This is a measurement that we use it to say how tall or long something is.
f   This is a hard material used for building.
g   This word means very big and tall in size.
h   When something is not old or traditional in style.

2 Four words from Activity 1 don't have definitions. Which words are they? Describe their meanings to a friend.

3 Read *As High As the Sky* again. Find words for each category.

Words for measurements and sizes: ...bigger...

Jobs: ....

Structures: ....

Names of famous structures: ....

4 What makes you remember a building? Use the ideas from the box.

age	architect	color
height		location
material	shape	use

Grammar 1

1   Watch Parts 1 and 2 of the story video. Where are they going to visit?

How tall is the Statue of LIberty?

2 Read the grammar box and complete.

Grammar

How tall is the Galata Tower?	It's 67 meters **tall**.
How long is the Great Wall of China?	It's 8,000 kilometers **long**.
How deep is the Atlantic Ocean?	It's 8,486 meters **deep**.
How far is Mexico City from New York?	It's 3,360 kilometers **away**.
.... is the Eiffel Tower?	It's 324 meters ....
.... is the Eurotunnel?	It's 50.45 kilometers ....
.... is the Mediterranean Sea?	It's 5,267 meters ....
.... is the Moon from the Earth?	It's 384,400 kilometers ....

3 Write questions for these answers. Then ask and answer with a friend.

1 ....
The Statue of Liberty is 93 meters tall.

2 ....
Route 66 in the United States is 3,945 kilometers long.

3 ....
Big Ben is 1,521 kilometers away from the Leaning Tower of Pisa.

4 Look, choose, and write.

deep   long   tall   wide

         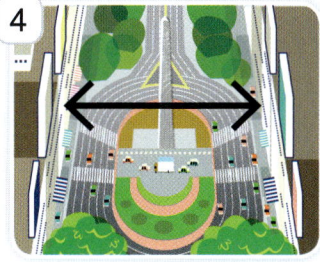

1	2	3	4
How long is the bridge? It's 244 meters.	_____ is the ocean? It's 3,500 meters.	_____ is the tower? It's 306 meters.	_____ is the street? It's three kilometers.

Speaking 1

Speaking strategy
Ask to find more information.

5 Choose three places or structures in your country. Find information and make notes.

6 Ask and answer questions with a friend about the places or structures. Complete the chart.

place/structure	tall	far	long	deep	wide	old

This is the Galata Tower. It's in Turkey.

How tall is it?

How old is it?

Pre-reading 2

1 Imagine you're planning your next vacation. Where are you going to go? Talk with your friends, then vote.

- a summer camp
- a city close to the ocean
- a city in the mountains
- an around-the-world trip

> **Reading strategy**
>
> Use clues in a text to make inferences.

2 Read and answer. Does Alma like playing sports? How do you know?

> Adela and Alma spend a lot of time together, both at school and after school. Alma is on the school hockey team and on the basketball team, and Adela always goes to the games to see her play.

3  Read *From Paris to Peru*. What do you think is in the package?

Reading 2

From PARIS to PERU

Last week, Rachel and Miriam were at Rachel's house making plans for their vacations.

"Where are you going to go this summer, Rachel? Have you decided?"

"I'm going to go to a summer art **camp** in France."

"France! That's wonderful, but … an art camp? What are you going to do there?" asked Miriam. "Are you going to be in Paris and spend the summer visiting art galleries? It doesn't sound very exciting to me."

"Well, we're going to visit Paris for a few days, but we're going to stay in the country and I'm going to do a lot of other things. Let me show you …" Rachel looked for some **brochures** and showed them to Miriam. "Here, look. I'm going to stay here, it's in a small town in the south of France. We're going to learn to draw and paint, and we're also going to learn about architecture, photography, and art history."

Miriam didn't look quite sure.

"Are you going to study all that in one month?" she asked.

"No, I'm not, not everything. I have to choose three, so I'm going to choose painting, art history, and architecture. Then I'm going to go on different excursions, for example, I want to see some of the small towns, so we're going to explore the **medieval** villages and draw, paint, and take pictures of them. There are some small **monasteries** where you can see beautiful **murals**. In one of the small towns, there's a very old tower with a beautiful **belfry**, a **staircase carved** in stone, and a **typical** garden surrounded by **arches**. I love old buildings and enjoy finding out about their history."

Rachel couldn't wait to go on vacation. Part of the art camp was a four-day excursion to Paris and she was really excited about this. There was so much to visit in Paris, the Eiffel Tower, of course – Paris' most important **landmark**. But also the Louvre Museum, the Arc de Triomphe, and many other things to see. The only thing she wasn't sure about was eating frogs' legs or snails!

After the summer, Rachel and Miriam got together at Miriam's house. Miriam had a lot of things on her bed from her vacation. There were clothes, socks, walking shoes, maps, a flashlight, a compass, sunblock, and pictures. She picked up a **package** and gave it to Rachel.

"This is for you. I'm sure you're going to love it." said Miriam.

"I love it, thank you!" smiled Rachel.

4 Would you like to go on vacation with Rachel? Why/Why not?

Comprehension 2

1 Read *From Paris to Peru* and Activity 2 again. What can you infer?

1 Who might be sporty?
2 What kind of vacation do you think Miriam would like to go on?

2 Read and circle.

1 Miriam and Rachel **have / don't have** the same interests.
2 Rachel **is / isn't** going to study all day on her vacation.
3 Children at the camp **are / aren't** going to see some old buildings.

3 Read and circle **T** (true) or **F** (false).

1 Rachel isn't interested in drawing.   T   F
2 An art camp isn't Miriam's favorite plan for her vacation.   T   F
3 Rachel is going to do a lot of different activities.   T   F
4 She's going to visit a lot of modern buildings.   T   F
5 She's only interested in visiting the Louvre Museum.   T   F

Listening 2

4 Imagine you're Miriam. What gift would you like to give Rachel?

Listening strategy

Listen for information to support my inferences.

5 (1-12) Listen and check your answer from Activity 4.

6 (1-13) Listen again and circle.

1 Miriam visited **one place / many places**.
2 The book is about a kind of architecture in **Peru / Spain**.
3 Miriam and her family **walked / flew up** to the architectural site.
4 When people don't want to walk to the site, you can take a **car / train**.
5 The **Romans / Incas** built the ancient site.
6 The architects in the book **used / didn't use** stone.

7 Discuss with a friend. Is it easy to take care of old buildings? Why are some buildings more difficult to take care of than others?

30

Vocabulary 2

1 Find these words in *From Paris to Peru*. Are they adjectives (**A**) or nouns (**N**)?

camp	......	mural	......
brochures	......	belfry	......
package	......	staircase	......
medieval	......	carved	......
landmark	......	typical	......
monasteries	......	arches	......

2 Read and answer. Use words from Activity 1.

1 Which four words describe a building or part of a building?

2 Which word describes a kind of artwork or painting?

3 Which word do you use to talk about a very famous structure?

4 When things are common or exactly like we think they will be, what are they?

3 Five words are missing from Activity 2. Which are they? Describe their meaning to a friend.

4 What kind of buildings did Miriam see in Peru? Are they similar or different from the buildings you read about earlier in the unit?

31

Grammar 2

1   Watch Parts 2 and 3 of the story video. Where's Doctor Who going to go?

The smogator is going to pollute the universe!

2 Look at the grammar box and read.

> ### Grammar
>
> **I'm going to do** a lot of different activities.
> You**'re going to travel** to Australia **next year**.
> Rachel **isn't going to spend** the whole day studying.
> My parents **are going to travel** to Spain for vacation **next** summer.
>
> **Are** you **going to study** all day? No, **I'm not**.
>
> **Going to** + verb refers to decisions taken before the time of speaking.

3 Read *From Paris to Peru* again. Circle examples of *going to*.

4 What are you going to do tomorrow? Complete the chart with three things you're going to do.

Three things I'm going to do tomorrow

5 Complete with the correct form of the verbs from the box.

| be | do | go | next | next year | see | study | travel | visit |

1 .... you .... to the United States .... summer?
Yes, I am. I .... New York. I want to see the Guggenheim Museum there.

2 Where .... Janis .... ?
She .... to Turkey. She .... the Galata Tower in Istanbul.

3 I want to go to Buenos Aires .... spring.
What .... you .... there?
I .... the 9 de Julio Avenue, it's the widest in the world.

4 What .... your brother .... next year?
He .... to university. He .... architecture.

Speaking 2

6 Plan a vacation for next summer with a friend. Decide where you're going to go and what you're going to do.

And what are you going to do on vacation?

I'm going to visit the Washington Monument.

Why are you going to visit that?

Because I like tall structures. I'm going to be an architect. What about you?

Writing

1 Scan the text. Answer the questions.

2 Read the text. Check your answers from Activity 1.

1 Why do tourists visit the house?
2 When was the building built?

The Falling Water House

The Falling Water House in Pennsylvania is a popular tourist attraction. Its design is very different and it's a National Historic Landmark. The architect Frank Lloyd Wright designed the house for a family to live in and it took three years to build, from 1936 until 1939 to construct the whole building.

The family loved mountains and nature so much that one of Frank Lloyd Wright designed the building to stand over a waterfall. It's beautiful! It's Frank Lloyd Wright's most famous pieces of work.

3 Read the text again and circle any numbers that add detail to the text.

4 Find or draw a picture of a famous house. Then go to the Workbook to do the writing activity.

Writing strategy

Use numbers, names, and facts to give detailed information, for example: *from 1936 until 1939*

34

Now I Know

1 Why are some buildings famous? Look back through Unit 2 and make notes.

Buildings:	Materials:
Measurements:	Historical places:
Landmarks:	Beautiful structures:

2 Choose a project.

Design a landmark for your school.

1 Imagine you're an architect. What structure would you like to design?
2 Brainstorm your ideas.
3 Draw your design.
4 Plan a presentation about your ideas and design.
5 Present your idea to the class.

or

Plan a tour of a city or town.

1 Work with some friends and choose a city or town.
2 Find information about important landmarks in your place.
3 Make a map of the places you're going to see on your tour and write notes.
4 Show your plan to the class.

Read and circle for yourself.

I can recognize a speaker's point. I can extract information about past events.

I can identify specific information. I can make basic inferences.

I can talk about personal experiences. I can talk about plans for the near future.

I can write descriptive texts about familiar places.

3

How can we protect wild animals?

Listening
- I can understand someone's reasons.
- I can recognize examples that support a speaker's point.

Reading
- I can understand basic opnions.
- I can understand the main ideas in simple stories.

Speaking
- I can talk about personal experiences.
- I can talk about past events or experiences.

Writing
- I can write short texts on familiar topics.

1 **Look at the picture and discuss.**

1 What can you see in the picture?
2 Where are the living things?
3 What do we mean by living things?
4 Can you name the living things?

2 **Read and make notes. Then compare your answers with a friend.**

1 What else do you know about the animals in the picture?
2 Is their habitat safe?
3 Should we protect animals? Why?
4 Do we need to protect their habitats?

3 3-1 BBC **Watch the video and answer the questions.**

1 What animal can you see at the beginning?
2 What is the second animal that you can see?
3 Why is the second animal in danger?
4 List some of the characteristics of this animal.

37

Pre-reading 1

1 💬 Discuss with a friend.

1 What do the animal facts make you think about?
2 What ideas does the text give you?

> **📖 Reading strategy**
>
> Think about the opinions expressed by the author in the text.

2 💡 Read and answer. How do you think the author feels about animals?

SAVE OUR ANIMALS!

Last month I watched a documentary about amazing animals on TV. I loved learning new things about tuna, gorillas, leopards, and turtles.

Sadly, many of them are now endangered and need our help. I think it's important to learn more about the endangered species and to teach everyone about the wonderful wildlife, birds, fish, and plants that live close to you.

3 🎧 Read *Once They're Gone, We Can't Bring Them Back*. What does the author want people to do?

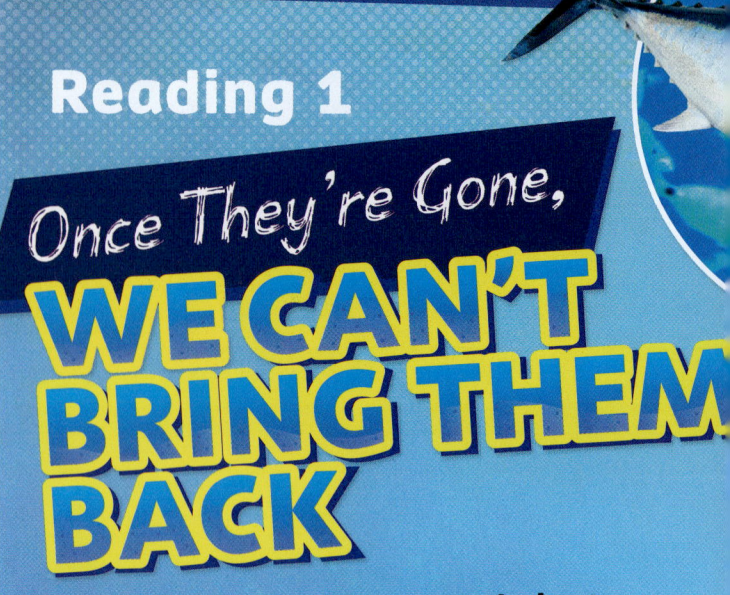

Reading 1

Once They're Gone, WE CAN'T BRING THEM BACK

There are many animals and plants on our planet that are in danger. Some animals, like the West African Black rhino, are now extinct. It's very sad that we won't see another animal from this species again. In the last 500 years, we've lost 869 species of plants and animals. They're now extinct.

There are also **species** of animals or plants that are **endangered**. This is because their **habitats** are changing, **disappearing**, are **destroyed**, or they're hunted by **poachers**. Some of these are well-known species, such as mountain **gorillas**, and scientists believe there are about 600 left in the **rainforests** of Congo and Rwanda, Africa. Animals like **snow leopards**, **bluefin tuna**, and sea turtles are all endangered, too.

38

Almost 100 countries in the world have **national parks**. These are protected areas for both animals and plants. Sadly, we can't protect sea animals like turtles in the same way. Over 25% of Costa Rica is national park, but in 1989 the golden toad became extinct. This teaches us that levels of pollution are getting worse. This is a dangerous time for living species in our seas and on land. How much can we help?

Today, almost all species of sea turtle are endangered, including the **leatherback turtle**. The leatherback is the largest of the sea turtles. An adult leatherback can weigh over 408 kilograms and grow as big as a small car! We can find these magnificent animals in the Pacific, Atlantic, and Indian Oceans … but how many of them are left? Well, it's difficult to know exact numbers, but we do know that the numbers of sea turtles are dropping.

The biggest problem for turtles and other sealife is that they eat tons of plastic. This plastic gets into oceans. There, things like plastic bags look like jellyfish to turtles. For some species of turtle, jellyfish are a form of food. This means they mistakenly eat the plastic bags.

Leatherbacks are born on land, but then live their whole life in the ocean. So, we need to find ways to stop our garbage and pollution from entering our oceans. We also need to **prevent** things like nets from fishing boats catching and trapping these beautiful animals. How much time do we have to change all that? Hopefully, enough.

> Let's save our sealife from extinction … and keep the sea trash free!

4 What habitats can you identify in your country? Which animals live in those habitats?

Comprehension 1

1 Check (✓) the sentence that best summarizes the text.

1 There are only a few turtles in the ocean. ☐
2 We need more national parks. ☐
3 We can't stop animals becoming extinct. ☐
4 We need to protect animals' habitats. ☐

2 Read *Once They're Gone, We Can't Bring Them Back* again and answer the questions. Then compare with a friend.

1 Where do these animals live?
- Leatherback turtle
  ....
- Mountain gorilla
  ....

2 What are two reasons why sea turtles are endangered?
....

3 Which two animals are extinct according to the article?
....

4 How are we destroying habitats?
....

Listening 1

3 A wildlife biologist studies wild animals and other wildlife. What questions would you ask a wildlife biologist?

🎧 Listening strategy

Listen for reasons that explain why something is happening.

4 🎧 1-15 Listen to a wildlife biologist talking to a group of children. What problem does she talk about?

5 🎧 1-16 Listen again and complete.

1 Some sealife thinks plastic .... like their food.
2 Plastic is dangerous for sea animals because they .... it.
3 We can .... large algae – it looks like seaweed.
4 This source of food .... on plastic.
5 Seabirds think the plastic is their ....

6 💬 Discuss with a friend. Why do you think other habitats, like rainforests, are in danger?

40

Vocabulary 1

1 Find these words in *Once They're Gone, We Can't Bring Them Back*. What do you think they mean?

> bluefin tuna   endangered   destroy
> disappear   gorilla   leatherback turtle
> national park   poacher   prevent
> rainforest   snow leopard   species

2 Match the words from Activity 1 to the definitions. Were your ideas correct?

1 This place is full of tall trees and it rains a lot there.
2 A person who catches and kills animals without permission.
3 This is a protected place where animals can live safely.
4 To no longer exist.
5 A plant or animal group.
6 This is the biggest kind of ape.
7 This animal lives in the ocean but starts life on land.
8 To stop something from happening or someone doing something.
9 To damage something so much that it no longer exists.
10 Animals or plants that are in danger of becoming extinct.
11 This is a fish that lives in the Atlantic Ocean.
12 This is a large cat that lives in Asia.

3 Discuss with a friend. Are there any endangered animals in your country? Why are they endangered? Do humans have a responsibility to protect wild animals and plants? Why?

Grammar 1

1 Watch Part 1 of the story video. Where's the man taking the animals? Then read and complete.

1 _____ _____ lions do you have?
2 _____ _____ money do you want?

2 Read the grammar box and write.

> **Grammar**
>
> **How many** animals were there in the cage?
> **How much** money is he going to make?
>
> 1 _____ milk do we have in the refrigerator? A lot!
> 2 _____ children did you invite to the party? Ten.
> 3 _____ protein is there in an egg? I don't know!
> 4 _____ bananas did you eat yesterday? Only one.
>
> countable   uncountable
>
> We use *How many* with _____ nouns.
> We use *How much* with _____ nouns.

3 Read *Once They're Gone, We Can't Bring Them Back* again and circle examples of *how many* and *how much*.

42

4 Write the words in the correct column.

bananas   bread   eggs   food   gorillas   milk
pictures   protein   snow leopards   water

How much … ?	How many … ?

5 Look, think, and write *How much* or *How many*. Then answer.

1 .... of Costa Rica is national park?

2 .... can leatherback turtles weigh?

3 .... mountain gorillas are there in Rwanda and Congo?

4 .... countries in the world have national parks?

5 .... plant and animal species have we lost in the last 500 years?

Speaking 1

6 Look and choose a topic. Then ask and answer with a friend.

Speaking strategy

Monitor your voice when talking about something exciting.

clothes   food and drink   pets

How many pets do you have?

One. I have a pet dog!

How much do you feed it?

A lot!

Pre-reading 2

1 💬 Discuss with a friend.

1. What's your favorite wild animal?
2. Where's its habitat?
3. What does it need to live?

> 📖 **Reading strategy**
>
> Look for the overall message the poem is trying to send.

2 💡 Read, think, and answer. Is the polar bear's habitat changing? What do you think the poem is trying to tell us?

Polar Bear

Dangerous, white
Arctic, cold.
I walk on ice
What a cold life.
I'm happy alone.
But it's too warm.
Slowly. Melting. My home.

3 🎧 1-17 Read *Where There's No Return*. Do you think the habitats and animals are safe?

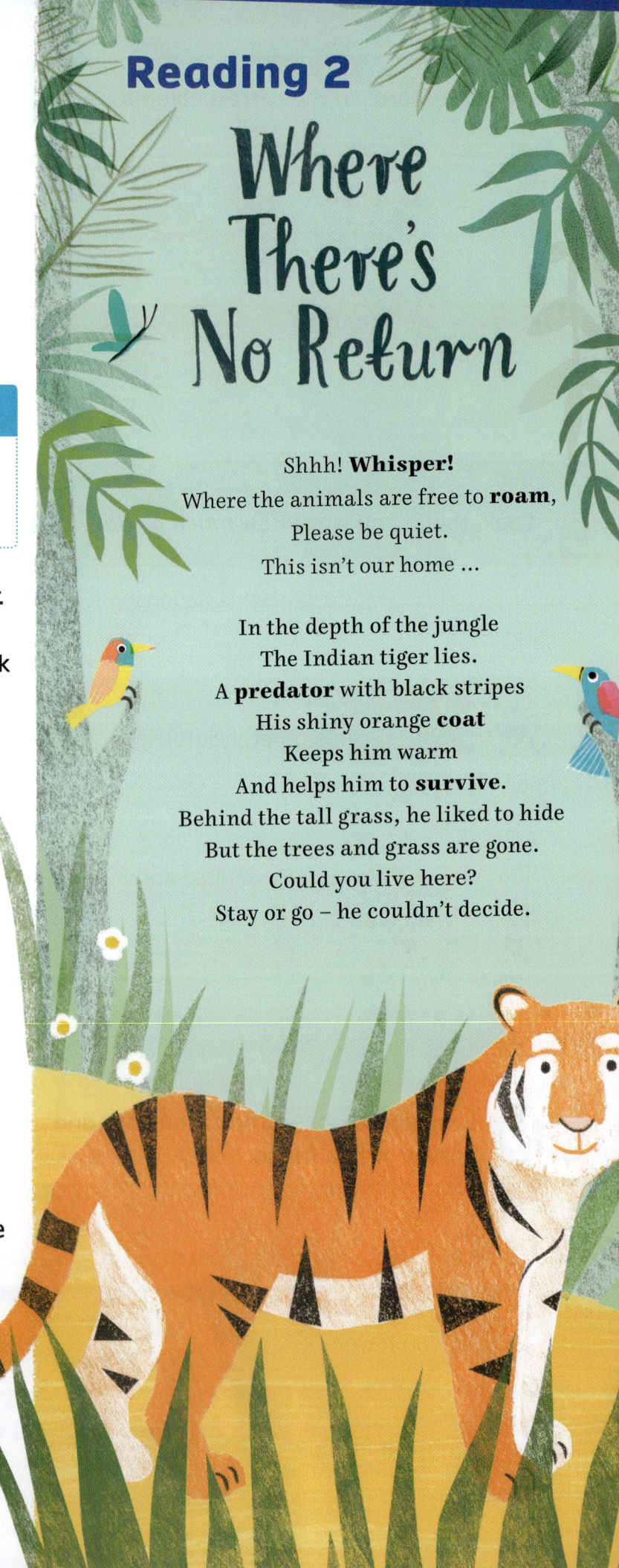

Reading 2

Where There's No Return

Shhh! **Whisper!**
Where the animals are free to **roam**,
Please be quiet.
This isn't our home …

In the depth of the jungle
The Indian tiger lies.
A **predator** with black stripes
His shiny orange **coat**
Keeps him warm
And helps him to **survive**.
Behind the tall grass, he liked to hide
But the trees and grass are gone.
Could you live here?
Stay or go – he couldn't decide.

44

Under the waves
Gracefully the turtle **glides**,
In and out of sea caves,
Around **corals** red and white.
Her hard, protective **shell**
She needs to survive.
Over rocks and with friends, she liked to play
But the water is dirty and dangerous.
Could you live here?
She couldn't stay.

High in the mountains, the pandas sit.
We like to sit and eat.
Hectares of trees and forest.
Not many of us are alive.
We need lots of our food,
We need to survive.
Delicious **bamboo**, we ate all day.
But now there are roads, our forest isn't here.
Could you live here?
We couldn't stay.

And you?
Have you got stripes,
Or spots or **tusks**?
Do you eat bamboo?
Do you live in the savannah?
In the ocean or sky?
And most importantly,
Do you need us to survive?

4 What do the animals in the poem have or need to survive? Do you think the animals are happy about their habitats changing?

Comprehension 2

1 Read *Where There's No Return* again. What do you think is happening to the animals' habitats?

2 Read again and answer. Then share your answers with the class.

1. How do the turtle's shell and the tiger's coat help them survive?
2. Why is bamboo important for the panda?
3. Who are the questions in the poem for?
4. Who's the last verse talking to?

3 Read and circle.

1. The turtle lives in **a cave** / **the ocean**.
2. There **is** / **isn't** a jungle in India.
3. There is **more** / **less** bamboo for pandas to eat.
4. Pandas **like** / **don't like** plants.
5. Humans and animals **need** / **don't need** each other.

Listening 2

4 What do you think about keeping wild animals as pets?

Listening strategy

Listen for examples used to support the speakers' points.

5 (1-18) Listen to the children. Check (✓) the topics you hear.

- rare animals ☐
- pandas ☐
- national parks ☐
- pets ☐
- starting a campaign ☐

6 (1-19) Listen again and circle **T** (true) or **F** (false).

1. The children like the poem. **T F**
2. Iguanas are exotic pets. **T F**
3. People don't have spiders as pets. **T F**
4. Some animals are endangered because they bite people. **T F**
5. The children will tell people about animal and habitat protection. **T F**

7 Discuss with a friend.

1. Do you think keeping exotic animals as pets is fair?
2. Are there any endangered animals in your country?

Vocabulary 2

1 Find these words in *Where There's No Return*. What do you think they mean?

> bamboo   coat   coral   glide
> hectare   polar bear   predator   roam
> shell   survive   tusks   whisper

2 Match the words from Activity 1 to the definitions. Were your ideas correct?

1 Parts of animals. ....
2 A kind of food. ....
3 A measurement of space or land. ....
4 The smooth movement though water or air. ....
5 To talk very quietly. ....
6 A large white animal. ....
7 To continue to live, especially if you're in danger. ....
8 To walk or move around and not have a clear plan of what to do. ....
9 They live in the ocean. They look like colorful rocks and plants. ....
10 An animal that hunts, kills, and eats other animals. ....

3 Read and circle one or two words.

1 We do this when we don't want to be loud.   **whisper / roam / survive**
2 These protect some animals.   **tusks / bamboo / shell**
3 Some land animals do this all day in their habitats.   **whisper / glide / roam**
4 A lot of these make a national park.   **tusks / predators / hectares**

4 Imagine you're organizing an animal protection day. How can we help animals? What information do you think is important to share?

Grammar 2

1 Watch Parts 2 and 3 of the story video. Where are they going to go? Why are the animals going on the spaceship?

"It's too late!"

They couldn't catch the alien animal collector.

2 Read the grammar box and circle.

Grammar

Look! I **can** run very fast!
Could you ride a bike when you were five?
I **couldn't** run fast when I was very young.

The Smogator **could / couldn't** escape.
The Doctor **could / couldn't** catch the poacher.

3 Read *Where There's No Return* again and circle examples of *could*, *couldn't* and *could + verb*.

4 Read and match.

1 My dad couldn't speak German when he was a child, but he
2 My mom's a great writer now, but she
3 My dad loved soccer. He couldn't play, but he
4 Jared and Sonia studied hard, but they

a could watch it for hours on TV.
b can now.
c couldn't spell very well when she was a kid.
d couldn't get good scores in science.

5 Read and complete. Use *can/can't* or *could/couldn't* and words from the box.

> play   send   watch

Zoey: Grandma, ¹ .... you .... emails when you were young?

Grandma: No, I ² .... There were no computers when I was young.

Zoey: And ³ .... your parents .... TV when they were young?

Grandma: Yes, they ⁴ .... And I ⁵ .... , too. We had a TV at home.

Zoey: And ⁶ .... you .... tennis when you were at school?

Grandma: Yes, I ⁷ .... And your Grandpa, too. We ⁸ .... tennis very well.

Zoey: I ⁹ .... tennis now, too.

Speaking 2

6 Work in groups. Write a questionnaire and ask and answer the questions. Then tell the class about your group.

	Speak English		
Me			
Friend 1			
Friend 2			
Friend 3			

Could you speak English when you were six?

Yes, I could, but I couldn't speak very well.

No, I couldn't, but I can now!

49

Writing

1 Scan the text. Find this information.

1. The name of the group.
2. Which species they want to help.
3. What they try to teach.

2 Read the text. Check your answers from Activity 1.

How Can You Help?

We are responsible for our country's wild animals, birds, fish, and plants. A good way to protect endangered species is to join an animal protection group.

Our group's name is *Our Animals* and we think about how animal habitats are in danger. We need to think about different ways to help. We care about monkeys, so we started this wildlife group to help them. We believe they need to be in the wild and not in people's homes. We try to teach people that monkeys aren't pets. You can help by visiting our monkey sanctuary and learning more about our work. You can also volunteer at the sanctuary and of course, we always welcome donations.

3 Read the text again and circle the connecting words.

4 **WB 43** Find or draw a picture of the animal the wildlife protection group helps. Then go to the Workbook to do the writing activity.

Writing strategy

We can connect words and sentences with **so**.
*We care about monkeys, **so** we started this wildlife group.*

Now I Know

1 How can we protect wild animals? Look back through Unit 3. Make notes on what you learned about these things. Add your own ideas.

- Endangered species
- Animal habitats
- Why they are in danger
- What we can do to help
- Exotic pets
- Sharing messages

2 Choose a project.

Find ways to protect wild animals

1. Think about five easy things you can do to protect wild animals.
2. Make notes and plan a presentation of these five things.
3. Present your ideas to the class.

or

Create a local habitat

1. Choose a habitat and research it.
2. Find or draw pictures that show the most important information.
3. Write some notes to explain what the pictures show.
4. Put your pictures and notes onto a poster and show it to the class.

Read and circle for yourself.

I can understand someone's reasons.
I can recognize examples that support a speaker's point.

I can talk about personal experiences.
I can talk about past events or experiences.

I can understand basic opinions. I can understand the main ideas in simple stories.

I can write short texts on familiar topics.

51

4
What can we do with our trash?

Listening
- I can understand details in dialogs.
- I can get the gist of recorded material.

Reading
- I can make basic inferences.
- I can predict what a text is about.

Speaking
- I can make suggestions about what to do.
- I can talk about personal experiences.

Writing
- I can write short texts on familiar topics.

1 Look at the picture and discuss.

1 What can you see in the picture?
2 Where does trash go when we throw it out?
3 What does recycling mean for you?
4 What materials can we recycle?

2 Read and make notes. Then compare your answers with a friend.

1 What sort of things can we recycle?
2 What are the benefits of recycling?
3 Do you recycle at home or at school?

3 Watch the video and answer the questions.

4-1 BBC

1 What does the person want to make?
2 What is she using to make it?
3 What does she use to make the tentacles and suckers?

🇬🇧 British	🇺🇸 American
rubbish	trash

53

Pre-reading 1

1 💬 **Discuss with a friend.**

1. What happens to the plastic we throw out?
2. Can we use less plastic and paper? How?

> 📖 **Reading strategy**
>
> Relate a text to the things you do in your life.

2 💡 **Read and answer. Are we recycling enough? How do you know?**

> Recycling is an excellent way to save energy and take care of the environment. Many countries in Europe recycle more than 50% of their waste, but hundreds of millions of tons of **plastic** and other waste are still sent to **landfills**. We all know that we should recycle plastic, but what happens to it when we just throw it out?

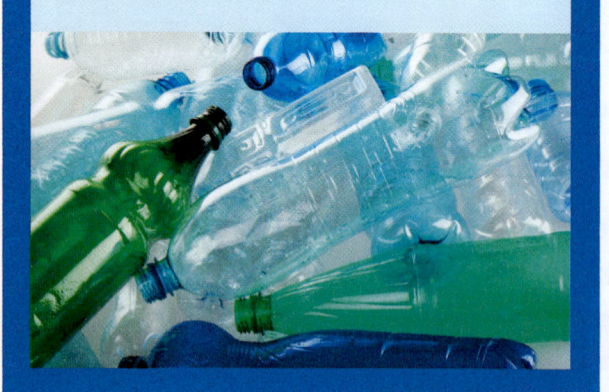

3 🎧 **Read** *Waste Not, Want Not!* **What do you do with the items after using them?**
1-20

Reading 1

WASTE NOT, WANT NOT!

We all know that we need to protect our planet. We know our wildlife and environment need our help, and we also know that we could do more as individuals to make a positive change.

Do you drink milk from plastic containers, soda from metal **cans**, or eat food from **glass jars**? Do you use writing paper or notepads? Most of us will answer "yes" to these questions, but the bigger question is, what can we do with these items to help our environment?

54

Ideally, we need to use **natural resources** to make more of our materials. This is because the process of creating plastic, **metal**, paper, or glass uses unnecessary energy and sends **toxic fumes** into the air. This all causes, and adds to, climate change. We know there's a big demand for this kind of **packaging**, so another way we can help is by not putting them in the general trash.

RRR

RRR – the Three Rs. We probably all know what these mean, especially *recycle*. But what about *reduce* and *reuse*? Let's use the example of plastic water bottles — there are about 50 kinds of plastic and we can recycle most of them. So, when we finish using a plastic bottle, we can clean it and then put it in the trash to *recycle*. It sounds simple, but over half of our plastic bottles are not recycled ... and this happens all over the world. To *reduce*, we could buy a larger bottle instead of a lot of smaller bottles. This could reduce the amount of packaging. Finally, we could easily *reuse* a plastic bottle. Once it's empty, fill it again and off you go. However, an even better idea is to use a reusable bottle. Then you don't need to buy throwaway plastic bottles!

Now, let's go back to *reuse*. Can you think of any other ways that we can reuse our plastic bottles? Maybe you have seen ideas for flower pots using old plastic bottles, **soil**, and plants. Or, birdfeeders filled with bird food. But what about clothes?

Clothes, from plastic bottles? Yes. There are some companies that use a **process** to make clothes from plastic bottles. First, they remove the caps and labels, clean the plastic and sort the different kinds or colors of plastic. Then, they crush and chop the plastic into very small pieces. This is melted and then they make long, thin fibers that can be used like cotton. These fibers are then used to make clothes. It's amazing and 25 plastic bottles can make one **fleece**. The fleeces are like any other sweater or jacket — they're warm and comfortable ... and these help us protect the environment!

4 Would you wear clothes made from recycled plastic? Why?/Why not?

55

Comprehension 1

1 Read *Waste Not, Want Not!* again. Check (✓) the answers for you. Then compare with a friend.

The article made me think about:

what I recycle ☐

how I can help produce less trash ☐

different things that we can make from trash ☐

anything else: ....

2 What's the main idea in the final paragraph?

1 An example of the benefits of recycling.
2 Pollution and how it can be reduced.
3 Reduce the plastic we throw away.
4 Causes of toxic fumes.
5 Reuse our clothes.

3 Read *Waste Not, Want Not!* again and complete the notes. Then compare your notes with a friend.

1 Turning natural resources into materials can produce *toxic fumes*.
2 We can .... things like metal, glass, paper, and plastic.
3 Toxic fumes in the air can cause ....
4 We can .... a plastic bottle by refilling it.
5 We can make a .... from 25 plastic bottles.
6 We can help the environment when we recycle, ..., and reuse.

Listening 1

4 What do you think a *Green Club* is? What activities can you do there?

> **Listening strategy**
>
> Make notes while listening to help you remember what you hear.

5 🎧 1-21 Listen and answer. What are they talking about?

recycling, collecting plastic bottles, ...

6 🎧 1-22 Listen again and make notes.

1 What did Shania's team do?
2 Which fruits or vegetables will they grow?
3 What is their main focus?
4 What are they planning?
5 What can people do?
6 What do we save if we buy things that aren't new?

7 💬 Discuss with a friend. Would you like to start a Green Club at your school? What would you like to do?

56

Vocabulary 1

1 Find these words in *Waste Not, Want Not!* Discuss their meaning with a friend. Which words are materials you can recycle?

> cans   fleece   fumes   glass jars   landfill   metal
> natural resources   packaging   plastic   process   soil   toxic

2 Read and circle.

1 A large space outside where you throw waste is a **landfill** / **natural resource**.
2 The stages you go through to do something is a **soil** / **process**.
3 An example of an item of clothing is a **can** / **fleece**.
4 Something that's dangerous to breathe in is **glass** / **toxic**.
5 Something that plants grow in is **soil** / **metal**.

3 Read *Waste Not, Want Not!* again. Find words for each group. Then compare with a friend.

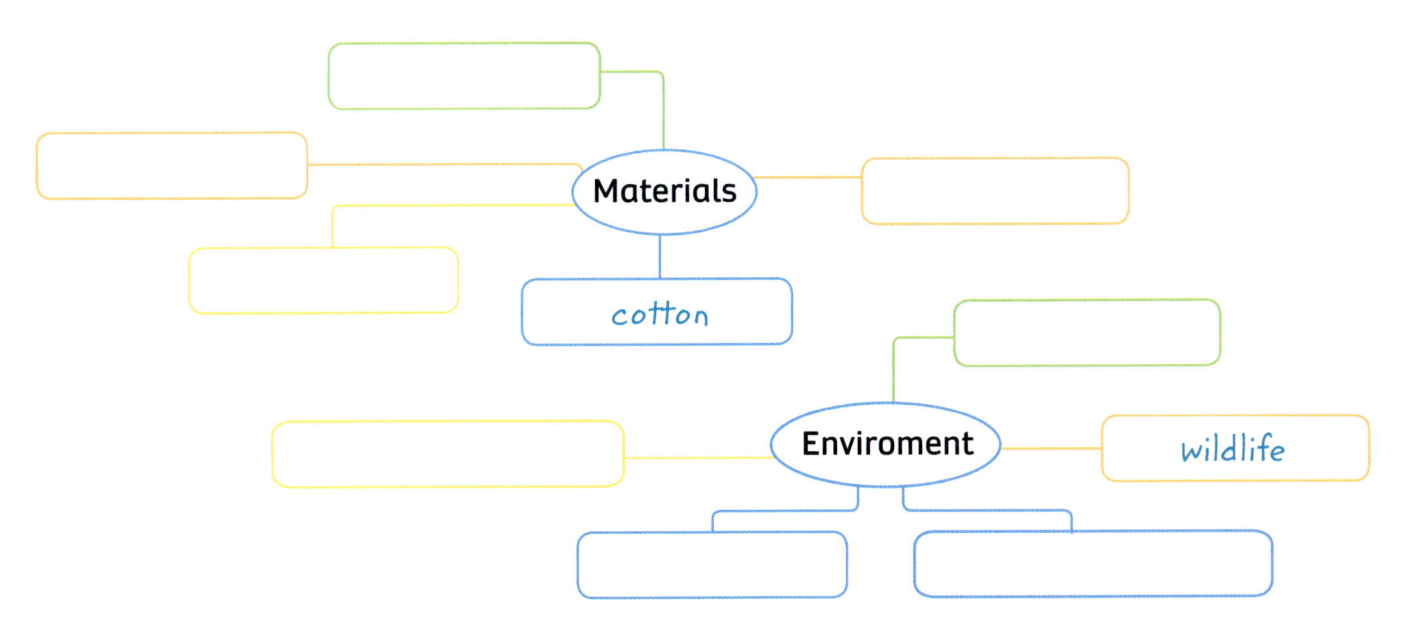

Materials: cotton

Enviroment: wildlife

4 What things are recycled at your school?
What things can be reused at your school or home?

57

Grammar 1

1 Watch Part 1 of the story video. What do they need to do?

2 Look at the grammar box and read.

> **Grammar**
>
> More people **need to** recycle more at home.
> You **don't need to** have a lot of money to start a Three Rs project at school.
> **Do** we **need to** use so much paper? No, we **don't**.

3 Read *Waste Not, Want Not!* again. Circle examples of *need to* and *don't need to do*.

4 Read and complete. Use *need to* or *don't need to* and the verbs in parentheses.

1 We're going to the beach today. You .... (bring) a hat and sunblock.
2 .... I .... (take) sunglasses?
3 We .... (buy) sandwiches. We're having lunch at a restaurant.
4 She .... (bring) her jacket. It's very warm and sunny.
5 They .... (use) glass bottles instead of plastic ones.
6 .... we .... (take) our jackets?
7 I .... (do) my homework today.
8 He .... (read) for tomorrow.

We **could make** a recycling plan for the school. What do you think?
Good idea! We **could reuse** last year's pencils.
Could we **ask** the older students to help us?
We use **could** to make suggestions and to talk about possible actions.
We never put the word *to* after **could**.

5 Read and complete. Use *could* and the verb in parentheses.

1 .... we .... (ask) the teachers to help us, too?
2 Our parents .... (take) the posters to the shopping mall.
3 .... the art teacher .... (help) us make the posters?
4 You .... (use) your old water bottle to make a pen holder.
5 Saira .... (make) a skirt from an old pair of jeans.

Speaking 1

6 Make a *Recycle, Reduce, Reuse* plan for your school. Think and discuss your ideas in a group.

What could we recycle?

We need to recycle more paper. We throw out paper every day.

We could make posters saying "We need to recycle paper!"

Pre-reading 2

1 💬 **Discuss with a friend.**

1. Do you reuse old things?
2. Is it possible to turn a piece of trash into something beautiful?

> 📖 **Reading strategy**
>
> Predict the kind of information you might find in a story.

2 💡 **Read, think, and answer. What do you think Ena's father creates?**

> When Ena and her sisters were small, their family had very little money. Their father made a new dining room table from an old door. The older children's clothes went to the younger children. Everyone was happy, but they wanted to make new things that were more fun. Ena's father was very creative and one day he had a totally new idea!

3 🎧 1-23 **Read *Rubbish Revival*. What's Rita's suggestion? What do you predict they'll do for Earth Day?**

Reading 2

RUBBISH REVIVAL

The school wanted to celebrate Earth Day and all the pupils started to plan their projects. Ahmed and his friends Rita, Luca and Jamie got together to make their plans. "Now, we all know the type of stuff that can be recycled like metal, glass, plastic, **cardboard** …" said Ahmed. "But what about all of the other stuff that we **throw out**? Isn't there something that we can do with all that? We throw away too much **stuff** every day and use too many plastic bottles!"

"Yes, you're right," replied Luca. "We know a lot about recycling, but all we do is learn about **recycling plants** and big things that we can't get involved with! What can we do at school and at home?"

"I know!" exclaimed Rita suddenly. "**Upcycling**!"

"Upcycling? What's that?" asked the boys. Rita sometimes had crazy ideas that only she could understand.

"It's making new things from rubbish." she said.

"But that's the same as recycling", said Jamie.

"No, it isn't." she replied. "When we recycle, we take things like plastic bottles or car **tyres**, and we make new products. For example, lots of plastic goes to a recycling plant and they then turn it into new plastic bowls or plastic **cups**, right?"

The boys nodded. Rita went on. "Upcycling is different. You take something, say … **toilet paper rolls**, for example. Then you cut and colour them, and **create** something completely and totally different … and pretty! Like the things we do with Miss Temple in arts and crafts!"

Rita switched on her laptop and searched the internet. She showed her friends some photos of upcycled things made from waste. There was some amazing jewellery made from paper and metal, and some cool **photo frames** made from cardboard. There were too many ideas to choose from.

"We could make **decorations** … for Earth Day!" said Luca.

"Or we could have an upcycle art competition!" said Jamie.

"Great ideas! We have enough rubbish. Let's plan what we're going to do," said Ahmed. "Rita, what do you think we need to do first?"

"I think we need to tell the other classes what upcycling is. We could also make a few things ourselves, and bring them to school … so they know what we're talking about. My grandma is a great upcycler. She made my pencil case from an old pair of denim jeans! She also used a chair – she used the old **wood** to make a box. I can ask her to help us."

Rita, Ahmed, Luca and Jamie worked very hard and their upcycled art competition was a great idea. Everyone in the school wanted to, and could, take part. It was so successful that they appeared in the local newspaper with some of the things everyone made!

4 How could you revive rubbish? Do you think it's a good idea to upcycle? Why?/Why not?

Comprehension 2

1 Read *Rubbish Revival* again. Who do you think was in the newspaper?

2 What do you think the story is mostly about?

1 Recycling and telling the school about how they can recycle.
2 Teaching the school about what upcycling is.
3 The competition in the local newspaper.

3 Read and answer. Then share your answers with the class.

1 Why is the story called *Rubbish Revival*?
2 Why did the children want to do a special project?
3 How do we know that the upcycling project was such a success?

Listening 2

4 What three questions would you ask Ahmed and Rita about their project?

> 🎧 **Listening strategy**
>
> Listen for the general context to help you find out meaning.

5 🎧 1-24 Listen and decide. Who's talking? What about?

6 🎧 1-25 Listen again and circle.

1 *Rubbish Revival* is **an art** / **a painting** competition.
2 The kids collected a lot of **cardboard boxes** / **different things**.
3 Kids could use **only plastic** / **different materials**.
4 The boys made **a sculpture** / **a bag**.
5 **Everyone** / **One class** took part in the competition.

7 💬 Discuss with a friend. What's the difference between recycling and upcycling?

Recycling is …   Upcycling is …

Vocabulary 2

1 Find these words in *Rubbish Revival*.
Circle the words for things you can upcycle.

| stuff | cardboard | cup | decorations | create | picture frames |
| recycling plants | tire | toilet paper rolls | throw out | upcycle | wood |

2 Match the words from Activity 1 to their definitions.

1 a place where you can turn waste into another thing ....
2 a variety of objects or things ....
3 to make something new, or invent something ....
4 we do this with our trash ....
5 like paper but harder ....
6 a car has four of these ....
7 this is in the bathroom ....
8 you drink water from this ....
9 something to put a picture in ....
10 paper is made from this ....
11 when you make something new from something old ....
12 things that look nice but have no use ....

3 💬 Think about the upcycled things you use or see every day. Then discuss with a friend. Where and what are they used for? Use the ideas from the box and your own.

| bottles | cans | picture frames | scarves | tires |

Let's …   Good point.   Anything else?
What about … ?   What kind of … ?
We can …   What do you mean … ?

63

Grammar 2

1 Watch Parts 2 and 3 of the story video. What's going to fall on Jack? Where does Jack say the glue could go? Then read and complete.

There's _____ trash!
There are _____ plastic bottles!
There's _____ space for everything!

Look at all this rubbish! Plastic bottles, metal cans, old bits of wood, broken bowls ...

2 Look at the grammar box and read.

> **Grammar**
>
> There's **too much** waste in the trash can.
> There are **too many** things in my bag.
> We don't have **enough** money to buy that book!
> Are there **enough** boxes to collect everything?

3 Read *Rubbish Revival* again and circle examples of *too much*, *too many,* and *enough*.

4 Read and complete.

| enough   too many   too much |

1 There's _____ bread, we bought more than we needed.
2 We don't have _____ boxes for everyone!
3 We're using _____ metal cans. We need to reduce what we use!
4 Do you have _____ milk in the fridge, Mom? I think we need more.

5 Read and complete.

1 I don't like the weather here. There's too _____ rain.
2 I have some, but not _____ money to buy the sandwiches.
3 Eight, nine, ten – great! I have _____ money now.
4 I can't drink this tea. I've put too _____ sugar in it!

Speaking 2

6 Think about situations where you can have too much and not enough of something. Make notes.

> **Speaking strategy**
> Think about the language you want to use.

When I eat too much birthday cake.

7 Discuss with a friend and use your notes.

There's too much cake!

I know, I've eaten enough cake!

65

Writing

1 Scan the text. What does Elinor want to do?

- remember to recycle more things
- reuse more things to help the environment
- buy new clothes

2 Read the text. Check your answer from Activity 1.

My Action Plan!

We produce a lot of waste around the world, but there isn't enough space on our planet for all of it. When we reuse things, we help keep the air clean, we save energy, and we reduce the toxic fumes that factories send into the air.

The things I can do to help are:

- use a reusable water bottle, so I don't throw away plastic bottles.
- give my old clothes to my younger sister or make them into something new!

3 Read the text again and circle examples of connecting ideas together.

4 **WB 57** Find or draw a picture for your action plan. Then go to the Workbook to do the writing activity.

Writing strategy

Use examples to support and connect your ideas.
*We produce a lot of waste around the world, **but** there isn't enough space on our planet.*

Now I Know

1 What can we do with our trash? Look back through Unit 4. Use the information you learned to complete the chart. Add your own ideas.

Materials	Actions	Places	Objects
plastic		landfill	

2 Choose a project.

Three Rs investigation

1. Find out what happens to the waste at your school.
2. Write a report using your results and ideas. Think about: what can be reduced, reused, or recycled.
3. Present your report to the class.

or

Create a piece of upcycled art.

1. Choose a piece of art you would like to make and make a list of the materials you will need.
2. Make your piece of art.
3. Present your work of art to the class.

Read and circle for yourself.

I can understand details in dialogs. I can get the gist of recorded material.

I can make suggestions about what to do. I can talk about personal experiences.

I can make basic inferences. I can predict what a text is about.

I can write short texts on familiar topics.

5

How can we choose our jobs?

Listening
- I can recognize a speaker's point.
- I can recognize a speaker's feelings or attitudes.

Reading
- I can scan texts for specfic information.
- I can infer about characters' feelings.

Speaking
- I can make comparisons between people or things.

Writing
- I can give facts to support an opinion.

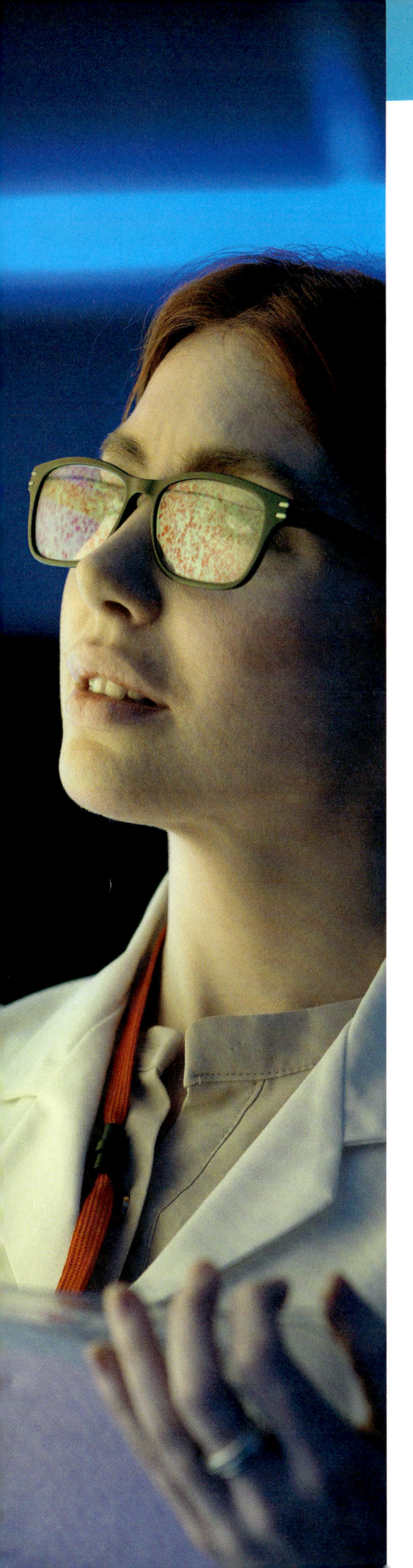

1 **Look at the picture and discuss.**

1 What can you see in the picture?
2 What job is she doing?
3 Would you like to do this job? Why?/Why not?
4 Do you know anyone who does a similar job to the woman in the picture?

2 **Read and make notes. Then compare your answers with a friend.**

1 What other jobs can you think of?
2 What job would you like to do? Why? Do you know anyone who already does this job? Have you asked them about it? What skills do you think you need to do this job?

3 **Watch the video and answer the questions.**

1 What do the two girls want to be?
2 What skills do you need for this job?
3 What does Ruth Jackson make?
4 What do the girls use?

69

Pre-reading 1

1 💬 **Discuss with a friend.**

1 Look at the people in the pictures. Which of these people do you know?
2 What do you know about them?

📖 **Reading strategy**

Compare the key details presented in different texts of the same kind.

---

2 Read and answer. What's a biography? Who is this biography about? Why is he famous?

Leonardo da Vinci

Leonardo da Vinci was one of the most important painters of the fifteenth century. His most famous painting is the *Mona Lisa*, a picture of a smiling woman. But Leonardo wasn't just a painter. He was also a scientist and an engineer – he designed a flying machine, a tank and a bridge, and he made drawings of the human body.

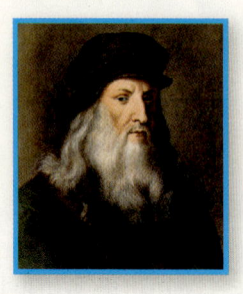

3 🎧 1-26 Read *Biographies*. What jobs did the famous people do?

70

Reading 1

Biographies

Jesse Owens
Born: 1913   **Died:** 1980

Jesse Owens was one of the world's greatest **athletes**. He was born in the USA, and had ten brothers and sisters. At school, he realised he could run faster than the other children. He wanted to be the best, so he **trained** very hard, and ran every day before school. In 1935, he set four world records in less than an hour! Then in 1936, he **competed** in the Olympics in Germany and won four gold medals in the 100 metres, 200 metres, the long jump and the 400-metre relay. After the Olympics, he didn't have much money, so he sometimes raced against horses, and won!

Ludwig van Beethoven

Born: 1770 **Died:** 1827

Ludwig van Beethoven was one of the greatest **musicians** of all time. He was born in Germany and learnt to play the piano when he was young. His father was a singer, and he was Ludwig's first music teacher. Ludwig was better at playing the piano than he was at reading and writing. He later lived in Vienna, where he played and **composed** music for piano and orchestra. When he was older, Beethoven's hearing became worse and worse until he was deaf and couldn't hear at all. He composed some of his best music after he became deaf.

Frida Kahlo

Born: 1907 **Died:** 1954

Frida Kahlo was one of Mexico's greatest **painters**. She had a difficult life because she was often sick. When she was 18, she was injured in a terrible bus accident and spent lots of time in bed getting better. This was one of the worst times of her life, but her mother got her an easel and some **brushes**. Frida started to paint and her bedroom was her **studio**. She is best known for her **self-portraits**, and her paintings are very colourful. One of her paintings shows her with her husband. He was also an artist.

Marie Curie

Born: 1867 **Died:** 1934

Marie Curie was born in Poland. She always wanted to be a scientist and when she was 24 she went to the Sorbonne University in Paris to study Physics and Maths. After university, she spent many hours in the science **lab** with her husband Pierre, who was also a scientist. They studied different materials and **discussed** the results. They **discovered** two new chemical elements: polonium and radium. In 1903, Marie Curie won the Nobel Prize for Physics. She was the first woman to get this prize and became very famous.

4 Why do you think these people did these jobs? Who do you think had the most interesting job? Why?

Comprehension 1

1 Read *Biographies* again and answer.

1. Who went to university? ....
2. Who didn't have a lot of money? ....
3. Who was injured in an accident? ....
4. Who couldn't hear? ....

2 Read *Biographies* again. Circle **T** (true) or **F** (false).

1. Frida Kahlo worked in a science lab.   T   F
2. Marie Curie was born in Poland.   T   F
3. Jesse Owens died when he was 67.   T   F
4. Ludwig van Beethoven stopped creating music when he became deaf.   T   F
5. Frida Kahlo's husband was a singer.   T   F
6. Beethoven's father was a teacher.   T   F
7. Jesse Owens competed in the 1936 Olympics.   T   F
8. Marie Curie always wanted to be a scientist.   T   F

Listening 1

3 What job would you like to do when you're older? Why?

> **Listening strategy**
>
> Listen for the reasons someone gives.

4 🎧 1-27 Listen and answer. What was Lena's dream job when she was a child? What job does she do now?

5 🎧 1-28 Listen again. Check (✓) the reasons why Lena loves her job.

1. Every day is the same. ☐
2. She travels all around the world. ☐
3. She gets to play some of the greatest music in the world. ☐
4. She meets a lot of interesting people. ☐
5. It's the most boring job in the world. ☐
6. It's a tiring job. ☐

6 💬 Discuss with a friend. What do you think is the most interesting thing about Lena's job?

72

Vocabulary 1

1 Find these words in *Biographies*. What do you think they mean? Discuss their meaning with a friend.

| athlete | brushes | compete | compose | discover | discuss |
| lab | musician | painter | self-portraits | studio | train |

2 Read and circle.

1. A musician **composes** / **trains** music.
2. An athlete **discusses** / **competes** in sports events.
3. A painter uses **brushes** / **a piano**.
4. A scientist **discovers** / **composes** new things.
5. A painter works in a **lab** / **studio**.
6. Scientists **compose** / **discuss** their results.

3 Read *Biographies* again. Write words connected with each job.

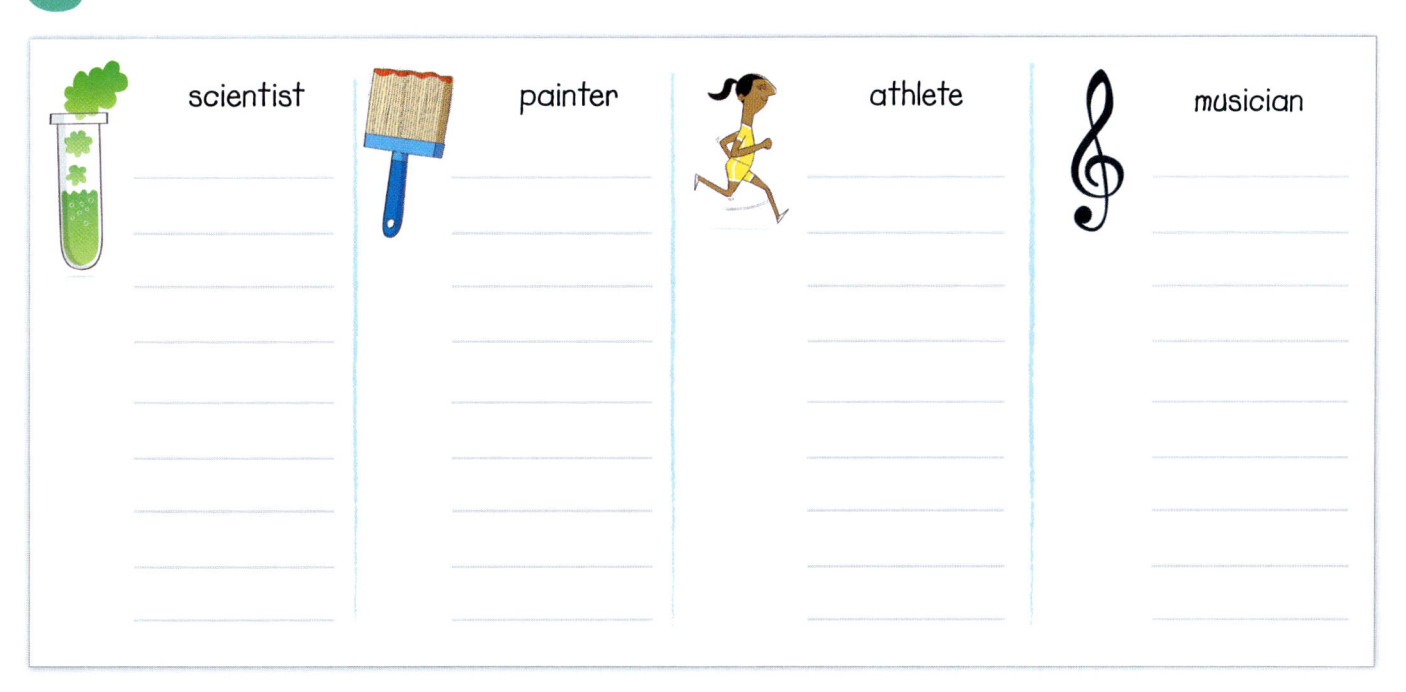

scientist	painter	athlete	musician

4 Which of these jobs would you like to do? Why? Discuss with a friend.

73

Grammar 1

1 Watch Part 1 of the story video. Answer the questions. Then read and complete.

> What did you think of that? Did I play .... or .... than before?

1 What's Jack's dream job?

2 Where do Jack and the Doctor go in the TARDIS?

2 Read the grammar box.

Grammar

Rashid runs **fast**. He runs **faster than** Santiago. He runs **the fastest** in our class.
Holy sings **loudly**. She sings **more loudly** than Dean. She sings **the most loudly** of all.

Jack played **well**. He played **better than** before. He played **the best**.
Roman played **badly**. He played **worse than** before. He played **the worst**.

1 The green words compare two actions.
2 The blue words describe actions.
3 The orange words compare all actions.

3 Read *Biographies* again and circle words that compare actions.

4 Read and circle.

1 Naiara runs **the most** / **more** slowly of all her friends.
2 Samuel speaks **more quietly** / **quieter** than Pablo.
3 Sofia did **better** / **well** in her math test this week than last week.
4 My old sneakers fit the **most comfortably** / **more comfortable** than all my shoes.

5 Complete the chart and write sentences with your own answers.

How well can you …

Write 1–5.
1 = really well   5 = not so well

play soccer?	☐	paint?	☐
play basketball?	☐	sing?	☐
speak English?	☐	do math?	☐
speak Spanish?	☐	do science?	☐
play the guitar?	☐	run?	☐
play the drums?	☐	swim?	☐

better   best   worse   worst

1 I play soccer well. I play it better than I play basketball.
2 ......
3 ......
4 ......
5 ......
6 ......

Speaking 1

6 Look at the actions in Activity 5. How well can you do them? Talk with a friend.

> **Speaking strategy**
> Think about what you want to ask.

athlete   clown   firefighter   musician
nurse   painter   scientist   singer

"How well can you play soccer?"

"I can't play soccer very well. I rated it five."

"I can play soccer better than you! I run fast and I score lot of goals."

75

Pre-reading 2

1 💬 Discuss with a friend.

1. Have you ever been on a long journey?
2. Where did you go? What was the journey like?

> 📖 **Reading strategy**
>
> Describe characters in a story and their feelings.

2 💡 Read and answer. Who do you think wrote this? What are they going to do? How do they feel?

> *Today, we're setting out on our journey. We're going to travel around the world faster than anyone before. I'm so excited, but a bit worried, too. It's going to be a long and dangerous journey, but I have my crew with me and we'll help each other. It'll be a great adventure!*

3 🎧 Read *Ahoy There!*. Where
1-29 does the boy go and why?

Reading 2

Ahoy There!

Day 1: *This is the most exciting day of my life! Today I'm traveling from my small town to join the crew of the* Golden Hind, *the fastest ship in all of England! My mom is worried. She says it'll be dangerous. But I'm not worried – I'm going on the greatest journey of my life, as a sailor and an explorer!*

Day 10: *I arrived at the ship and met our Captain, Sir Francis Drake. He's the greatest explorer of our time! There are 80 men in the crew, and they're all older than me – I'm 15 so I'm the youngest, but I don't mind. I'm going to travel around the world and it's going to be much more exciting than life in the small town!*

76

My bed is some straw on the floor. It isn't very **comfortable**, and I think it'll be cold and damp. My bed at home is more comfortable ... but I'm still happy to be here!
We bought food and water before our journey. We have some meat, butter, and cheese. And there's some bread and biscuits. Then we set off, sailing on the ocean. There are five other ships sailing with us, but they're smaller and slower than this ship. This ship sails so **fast**, it's incredible!

Day 90: After three months on the ocean, I'm feeling hungry and thirsty. Yesterday, we didn't have any meat or vegetables left for dinner, so we ate dry bread. And we don't have much fresh water left. There isn't enough water for washing, so we're all dirty and smelly. I'm much dirtier than normal.
We work very **hard** every day. We get up early, work all day, and go to sleep very **late**. I'm so tired ... I'm missing home and I'm a bit worried now about this journey.

Day 100: Yesterday, there was a terrible storm. It was the most terrifying experience of my life. The ship was like a little toy on the huge waves. We still don't have much food and I'm hungrier and thirstier than before. Some of the men are getting sick and there isn't a doctor or **surgeon** on the ship to help them – just the **barber**, who usually cuts our hair. He tries to help the men who are sick, but he can't do much.

Day 120: Today, I'm much happier because we reached the coast of Africa. We're a long way from home, but the ocean is calmer and it's hot! It's much hotter than in England. And we have fresh food to eat! They have the most **delicious** food here – bananas, limes, and coconuts. Yesterday we caught some fish and the cook made us a wonderful dinner of fish and potatoes. Our stomachs are full and we're all happier. I'm starting to think this journey is fun again!

4 How can you describe the boy in the diary?

Comprehension 2

1 Read *Ahoy There!* again and answer.

1. How does the boy feel at the start of his journey?
2. How does his mom feel?
3. Do his feelings change during the journey? How?

2 Read and answer. Then share your answers with the class.

1. What was the *Golden Hind*?

2. Where did the crew sleep on the ship?

3. Why were the crew hungry?

4. What other problems did they have during the journey?

5. How did the boy feel at the end of the story? Why?

3 Find words and phrases in *Ahoy There!* that describe the boy's feelings about the journey.

Good feelings	Bad feelings
excited	hungry

Listening 2

> **Listening strategy**
> Listen for key information about people.

4 🎧 1-30 Listen and check (✓). Which two people are speaking?

an explorer ☐   a scientist ☐
a photographer ☐   a sailor ☐
a reporter ☐

5 🎧 1-31 Listen and circle **T** (true) or **F** (false).

1. Malavath Poorna was the first girl to climb Mount Everest.   T   F
2. Her biggest problem was feeling cold.   T   F
3. The thing she missed most was her bed.   T   F
4. Her biggest dream now is to become a nurse.   T   F

6 💬 Discuss with a friend. Would you like to go on a similar expedition to Malavath's? Why?/Why not?

Vocabulary 2

1 Find these words in *Ahoy There!*. Circle the words for jobs and underline the describing words.

> barber   comfortable   crew   delicious   explorer   fast
> hard   journey   late   sailor   surgeon   terrifying

2 🎧 1-32 Listen to the meanings and say.

3 Read and match.

1. Someone who travels to find new places is an
2. Someone who sails on a ship is a
3. A doctor who fixes things inside the body is a
4. Someone who cuts hair and beards is a
5. A group of people who work together on a ship are the
6. To travel from one place to another you go on a

a. crew.
b. journey.
c. sailor.
d. surgeon.
e. explorer.
f. barber.

4 💬 Imagine you're an explorer from the past. Work with a friend and describe your journey. Then tell the class.

1. How did you travel? Where did you go?
2. What happened during your journey?
3. How did you feel during your journey?
4. What adjectives can you use to describe the journey?

Grammar 2

1 🎬 5-3 BBC Watch Parts 2 and 3 of the story video. Answer the questions. Then read and complete.

1 What's the photographer doing?
2 Who started the fire?
3 Who's going to help the firefighters stop the fire?

> The poor firefighters. They really are working hard. They have the .... difficult job.

2 Read the grammar box.

Grammar

Adverbs describe actions

The firefighters are working **hard**.
They're working **harder than** the reporter.
They're working the **hardest**.

The firefighters work **carefully**.
They work **more carefully than** the reporter.
They work **the most carefully**.

Adjectives describe things

The fire is very **big**.
It's **bigger than** any other fire.
It's **the biggest** fire in Australia.

The photographer has a **difficult** job.
She has a **more difficult** job than the reporter.
The firefighters have the **most difficult** job.

3 Read *Ahoy there!* again and circle -er and -est words.

4 Read and circle.

1 The firefighters work **careful** / **carefully**.
2 Traveling by plane is **safer** / **more safely** than traveling by bus.
3 This is the **loudest** / **loudly** class in the entire school.
4 My mom always drives very **slowly** / **slow**.

5 Read, look, and complete.

> big   building   difficult   dry
> fast   planet   quick   tall

1 The Burj Khalifa is .... in the world.

2 The Atacama Desert is .... in the world.

3 Jupiter is .... in the solar system.

4 The Amazon flows ....

5 The snake moves .... the tortoise.

6 A climber of Annpurna has .... job.

Speaking 2

6 Use the words in bold to compare the jobs.

Maya: My dream is to be a teacher. What's your dream job, Lola?

Lola: My dream is to be a reporter. It's a really **interesting** job. A reporter ¹ *writes more interesting* stories than a teacher! How about you, Sam?

Sam: My dream is to be a firefighter. Firefighters are **strong**. I think they're ² .... teachers and reporters.

Maya: But being a firefighter is **dangerous**. It's ³ .... being a teacher.

7 What's your dream job? Compare your dream job with a friend.

81

Writing

1 Scan the text. Answer the questions.

1. What does the writer want to be?
2. Give two reasons why.
3. Is this a job you'd like to do? Why?/Why not?

2 Read the text. Check your answers from Activity 1.

My DREAM Job

My biggest wish is to be a musician because I love music! I'm good at singing and I compose my own songs. I think they're quite good! I'm also working hard to learn to play the guitar and the piano. My best instrument is the violin. I started learning when I was six years old and I am pretty good! I play in the school orchestra. I think being a musician is more exciting than any other job because you can play music every day and you can meet other people who like music, too. I hope that one day I'll record one of my own songs in a music studio. I think being a musician is the best job in the world!

3 Read the text again and circle phrases that express opinion.

4 (WB 71) Find or draw pictures of your dream job. Then go to the Workbook to do the writing activity.

Writing strategy

State an opinion about a job and give reasons to support it.
I think being a musician is more exciting than any other job because you can play music every day.

Now I Know

1 How can we choose our jobs? Look back through Unit 5. Use the information you learned to answer the question. Add your own ideas.

When we choose a job, we think about
- what we're good at.
- what we like doing.

....

....

2 Choose a project.

Create a questionnaire

1. Make notes about four or five jobs and what you need for each one.
2. Create a questionnaire with questions about what people like and what they're good at.
3. Give the questionnaire to your classmates.
4. Present their answers in class and suggest a job for each person.

or

Create a biography

1. Choose a famous scientist, explorer, athlete, musician, photographer, or painter.
2. Find out as much as possible about their life.
3. Write a biography using the information you found. Add some pictures showing important things in the person's life.
4. Present your biography in class.

Read and circle for yourself.

I can recognize a speaker's point and feelings or attitudes.

I can make comparisons between people or things.

I can scan texts for specfic information.
I can infer about characters' feelings.

I can provide facts to support an opinion.

83

6

What happens in extreme conditions?

Listening
- I can identify key points in facts.
- I can extract information about past events.

Reading
- I can identify the structure of texts.
- I can make basic inferences.

Speaking
- I can express my opinion.

Writing
- I can describe the plot of a movie or book.

1 **Look at the picture and discuss.**

1. Where do you think the people are?
2. Why are they dressed like that?
3. How do you think they feel?

2 **Read and make notes. Then compare your answers with a friend.**

1. What kind of character do you think you need to climb in extreme conditions?
2. Do you think these people have to train to be able to go on expeditions like these?
3. Have you ever been in the mountains? Did you wear special clothes?

3 **Watch the video and answer the questions.** (6-1 BBC)

1. What does "Ice Man" not feel?
2. What's the first activity they try?
3. Does the "Ice Man's" heart get faster in the cold?
4. Is it usually dangerous to run in very cold weather?

85

Pre-reading 1

1 💬 Discuss with a friend.

1 What's the climate like in Antarctica? And in the desert?
2 Can extreme temperatures and weather be dangerous?

> 📖 **Reading strategy**
>
> Identify how texts are organized.

2 💡 Read and answer. What did Orellana find? What kind of text do you think this is? How do you know?

Book: City of Gold
⭐⭐⭐⭐⭐

Francisco de Orellana was a Spanish explorer, and the first person to sail the Amazon river. Orellana and his men wanted to find the lost city of El Dorado because they thought there was a lot of gold there. They started their journey in February 1542, but they never found the city. They found the Amazon, but Orellana and his men didn't know the dangers they were going to find along the way.

3 🎧 2-01 Read *Extreme Climates!*. Discuss with a friend.

1 What's the first paragraph about?
2 What are the other parts of *Extreme Climates!* about?

Reading 1

EXTREME CLIMATES!

By Caterina Lopez

I spoke to Jason Hewitts (documentary maker) about his latest documentary to be aired later this year. The documentary looks at extreme climates across the world. Jason starts in Antarctica and talks about Roald Amundsen's expedition.

The climate of Antarctica is the coldest on Earth. Here, the weather can be too cold to go outside. These **extreme** weather conditions are dangerous for humans. Our bodies are simply not designed for them. Most of us live in places with **mild** temperatures. Only a few people, like the Inuit in Arctic Canada and the Nenets in the north of Russia can **adapt to** these temperatures. This episode goes back to the 1900s when Amundsen and his men prepared for their greatest adventure.

Our hands, feet, ears, and nose can start to feel **numb** and turn blue when our body loses heat faster than it produces it. This is called **hypothermia**. When this happens, your breathing and **heart rate** get faster. You start to **shiver** as your body tries to keep warm. Your skin becomes cold and pale, and muscles become tight and hard. This is dangerous because we can also feel **dehydrated**. Our episode this week shows us the dangers that Amundsen and his team experienced on their polar journey. Don't miss it!

Extremely hot weather is dangerous, too. We all **perspire** when our bodies keep us cool. But our body can become dehydrated when we produce a lot of **sweat**. You might have a headache and in extreme heat your heart will **beat** very fast. In extreme heat, it's also possible to suffer from **heatstroke**. When this happens, you must see a doctor.

One of the hottest places on earth is *Death Valley National Park*. What dangers do people who live and work in the desert have? In our Sunday episode, we'll follow the Timbisha Shoshone tribe, who live there!

Our summers are getting hotter and hotter, and there are many places around the world where the temperature can go up to 45° C and more. There are also times when there's unexpected cold weather – and we aren't prepared. That's why we must be careful, especially with small children, babies, and older people. In this episode, we talk to Dr. Helena Smith about what we have to do when we experience extreme temperatures in our everyday lives.

4 Which episode would you most like to watch? Why? How do you feel when you are too hot or too cold?

Comprehension 1

1 Read *Extreme Climates!* again and answer. Then compare your answers with a friend.

1 How many episodes are there?
2 Which episode tells you more about living in Death Valley?

2 Read the titles. Which paragraph from the text do they refer to? Write the number.

1 Ice cold danger ☐
2 Daily dangers ☐
3 Can't take the heat ☐
4 The journey starts ☐

3 Read *Extreme Climates!* again and circle.

1 The weather in Antarctica is **wet** / **cold**.
2 **Only a few people live** / **Nobody lives** in polar areas.
3 Hypothermia happens when your body can't **keep warm** / **cool down**.
4 We can dehydrate in **extremely hot weather** / **extremely cold and hot weather**.
5 We perspire because **our body is trying to stay cool** / **we are shivering**.
6 You can have heatstroke **only in a desert** / **anywhere** when the temperature is high.

Listening 1

4 What extreme weather happens where you live? How can you prepare for it?

> **Listening strategy**
> Identify what you're listening to and listen for important points.

5 🎧 2-02 Listen and answer. What is it? Which words helped you decide?

6 🎧 2-03 Listen again and answer. Then compare your answers with a friend.

1 Where's the cold air coming in from?
....
2 How many countries are mentioned?
....
3 Where's it going to be extremely cold?
....
4 Where's it difficult to sleep at night?
....
5 What do these numbers refer to?
 -15 ....
 45 ....
 110 ....
6 What do you do when there is a tornado?
....

7 💬 Discuss with a friend. How can you protect yourself and others in any of these situations?

Vocabulary 1

1 Find these words in *Extreme Climates!*. Then complete the chart.
Can you think of any more words to add?

| adapt to | beat | dehydrated | extreme | heart rate | heatstroke |
| hypothermia | mild | numb | perspire | shiver | sweat |

Weather words	Effects of extreme temperatures

2 Match the words from Activity 1 to the definitions.

1 Our body produces this when we're hot.

2 This is when a part of our body can't feel.

3 When we change to help us survive.

4 Our heart needs to do this.

3 Think about what you learned in *Extreme Climate!*. Make notes.
Then present to the class.

Do this in the winter	Don't do this in the winter
wear warm clothes	
Do this in the summer	**Don't do this in the summer**

4 How do you think extremely cold or extremely hot weather can affect our planet? How can this affect our lives?

Grammar 1

1 Watch Part 1 of the story video. Answer the questions.

> Put on extra gloves and socks. You must be careful with your fingers and toes.

1. Why must they be careful with their fingers and toes?
2. Why does Jack need to look after his fingers?
3. What's wrong with the weather?

2 Look at the grammar box and read.

Grammar

I **must** find the Smogator.
You **must** wear gloves, it's cold.
Must you make that noise?

I **have to** take my exams.
You **have to** wear a seat belt.
Do we **have to** finish the project today?

Must expresses obligation that comes from the speaker (not a rule or a law).
Have to expresses obligation that comes from somebody else (can be a rule or a law).

3 Read *Extreme Climates!* again. Circle examples of *must* and *have to*.

4 Read and complete. Use *must* or *have to* and the verbs in parentheses.

1. _____ you _____ (wear) a uniform to go to school?
2. Look! An accident! We _____ (call) the police!
3. We _____ (buy) some food for dinner.
4. I can't go out now. I _____ (start) my science homework.

5 Read and complete. Then check (✓) the things that you don't have a choice about doing.

1 I _____ go to school tomorrow. ☐
2 I _____ go to the movies with my Grandpa tonight. ☐
3 I _____ eat breakfast in the morning. ☐
4 I _____ brush my teeth every day. ☐
5 I _____ play badminton tomorrow. ☐
6 I _____ do my homework this afternoon. ☐

6 Read and complete. Use *must* or *have to* and words from the box.

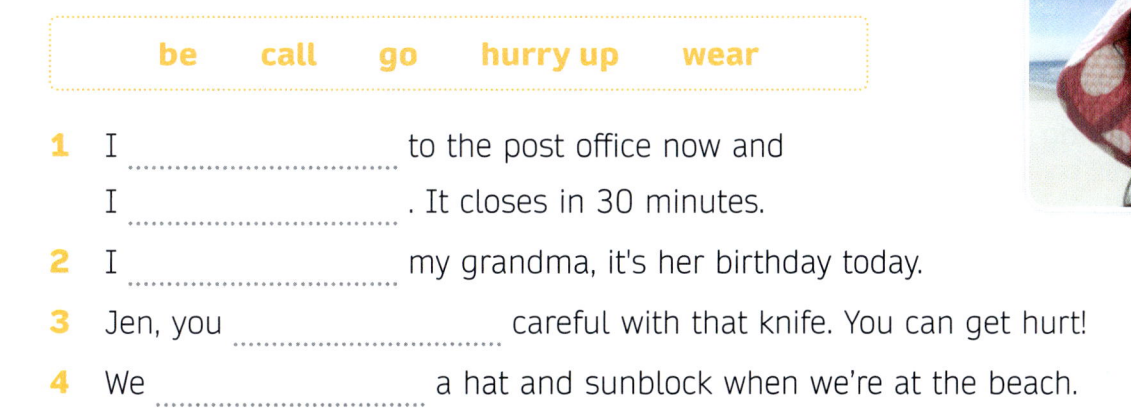

| be | call | go | hurry up | wear |

1 I _____ to the post office now and I _____ . It closes in 30 minutes.
2 I _____ my grandma, it's her birthday today.
3 Jen, you _____ careful with that knife. You can get hurt!
4 We _____ a hat and sunblock when we're at the beach.

Speaking 1

7 💬 What important things do you have to do in extreme weather conditions at school? Discuss with a friend.

What do we have to do at school when there's a storm?

When it's too wet to go outside, we must stay inside.

And we have to shut the doors and windows.

91

Pre-reading 2

1 💬 Discuss with a friend.

1. Do you know any kinds of natural disasters?
2. What can you do to prepare for a natural disaster?

> 📖 **Reading strategy**
>
> Use what you already know to identify problems and solutions.

2 Read and answer. What's the problem? How do you know?

> My friend Leyla and I were sitting under a tree in the playground during a break. We were far away from the other children because we were reading our notes for our science test. Suddenly, the birds stopped singing. I don't know why, but I knew something was going to happen ... and then the rain started!

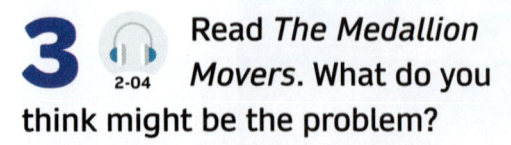

3 🎧 2-04 Read *The Medallion Movers*. What do you think might be the problem?

Reading 2

The MEDALLION MOVERS

"I wonder where we are," asked Miranda. "This place is incredible. Wow, look at those fountains and sculptures, and the gardens! Look at the people. They're wearing tunics and sandals. And look at the buildings. This is amazing, look, they're ..."

"Hey! Miranda. Stop for a second. You don't have to talk all the time! Your **medallion** is shining, look. It'll show us where we are and how far back in history we travelled," replied Tomás. Miranda looked at her medallion. "Oh yes. I forgot to check it!" It showed Italy, 24th August, 79 AD. "Ooohhh." Suddenly, she felt a little scared.

"What's wrong? 24th August, 79 AD. What does that mean?" asked Tomás. "Are you OK, Miranda? You look frightened, pale, and you're shaking. You don't have to be scared."

Miranda was looking at something behind Tomás. He turned around and saw a big mountain not far from the city. There was a strange cloud over it. "I think I know exactly where we are ... see that mountain over there? It isn't a mountain, it's a massive **volcano**. We mustn't panic!" But Miranda sounded worried.

Tomás started searching for information on his smartphone and quickly found something. "OK, I found the information! Here!" he exclaimed, "24th August, 79 AD. It's today, 24th August in the year 79. This is Pompeii, wow, we're in Pompeii ... and that's Vesuvius! OK, now I understand why you're scared. I'm pretty sure there's going to be an **eruption**! We have to escape, right away! We're probably **in danger**!"

Suddenly, there was a loud noise, a deep rumble like thunder, and thick grey smoke started to bubble and spill from the volcano's **crater**. "We have to tell everyone!", shouted Miranda. She ran towards a group of people. "You mustn't stay here!" she said. They said something, but she couldn't understand the language. She told them to run away, but they didn't understand her. Suddenly, they felt a **tremor**, and then another. The tremors **shook** the ground beneath them. They shook the city and some of the tents in the market square **collapsed**. People felt scared, but were prepared and ran to their families and houses.

Tomás pointed in the opposite direction. "Let's go up to those hills. They're far from the volcano ... and the **lava** will come down here, but we'll be **safe** up *there*," said Tomás.

They started to run, but suddenly there was another huge **explosion**. The sky was very dark with smoke now and people were running everywhere. Hot stones and **ash** flew out of the crater and fell everywhere, like rain. They fell on to the houses and temples. There was fire everywhere too — the hot stones and ash were too hot to touch.

"Too late! It's erupting!" shouted Miranda. She could feel her heart beating faster and faster. Suddenly, a group of people ran past them. One boy stopped and said something to Miranda. It looked like he was scared too.

"What did he say?", asked Tomás.

"Sorry, I can't understand what he's saying. He's speaking Latin," said Miranda. The boy pointed in another direction and waved for them to follow.

"To the sea!" exclaimed Tomás. "Of course! He's pointing to the sea. We'll only be safe in the sea! Let's follow him!"

4 Imagine you're in Pompeii with Tomás and Miranda. What would you do?

Comprehension 2

1 Read *The Medallion Movers* again. Why does Tomás think they're going to be safe in the sea?

2 Read and answer. Then share your answers with the class.

1. What's the story about?
2. When and where does it happen?
3. What helped Miranda and Tomás know where they were?
4. What's special about the medallion?
5. What information do you think you can find using Tomás's phone?

3 Read and number the events in the order they happen.

The children told people about the danger.	☐
The medallion showed a date.	☐
Miranda realized where they were.	☐
Miranda and Tomás arrived in the city.	1
The boy spoke to the children.	☐
Smoke came out of the volcano.	☐
Tomás found the information.	☐
The children started to run to the hills.	☐
An eruption started.	☐

Listening 2

Listening strategy

Listen for a change in events by listening for new names, numbers, and places.

4 🎧 2-05 Listen and check (✓) the main changes to the story's ending.

1. Tomás and Miranda made a new friend. ☐
2. The boy found his family and they leave. ☐
3. Tomás and Miranda traveled to Costa Rica. ☐
4. Pompeii was covered in smoke. ☐

5 🎧 2-06 Listen again and circle **T** (true) or **F** (false).

1. The boy knew the man in the white tunic. **T F**
2. The man and the woman were the boy's family. **T F**
3. Tomás and Miranda traveled to Costa Rica on the ship. **T F**
4. They time traveled to another volcano in Costa Rica. **T F**
5. Tomás and Miranda weren't scared about the volcano called Cerro Chato. **T F**
6. They decided to go and explore Italy. **T F**

6 💬 What might happen next in the story? What do you think they will say and do?

Vocabulary 2

1 Find these words in *The Medallion Movers*. What do you think they mean? Which words are kinds of movement?

> ash   collapse   crater   eruption   explosion   in danger
> lava   medallion   safe   shake   tremor   volcano

2 Label the picture. Use words from Activity 1.

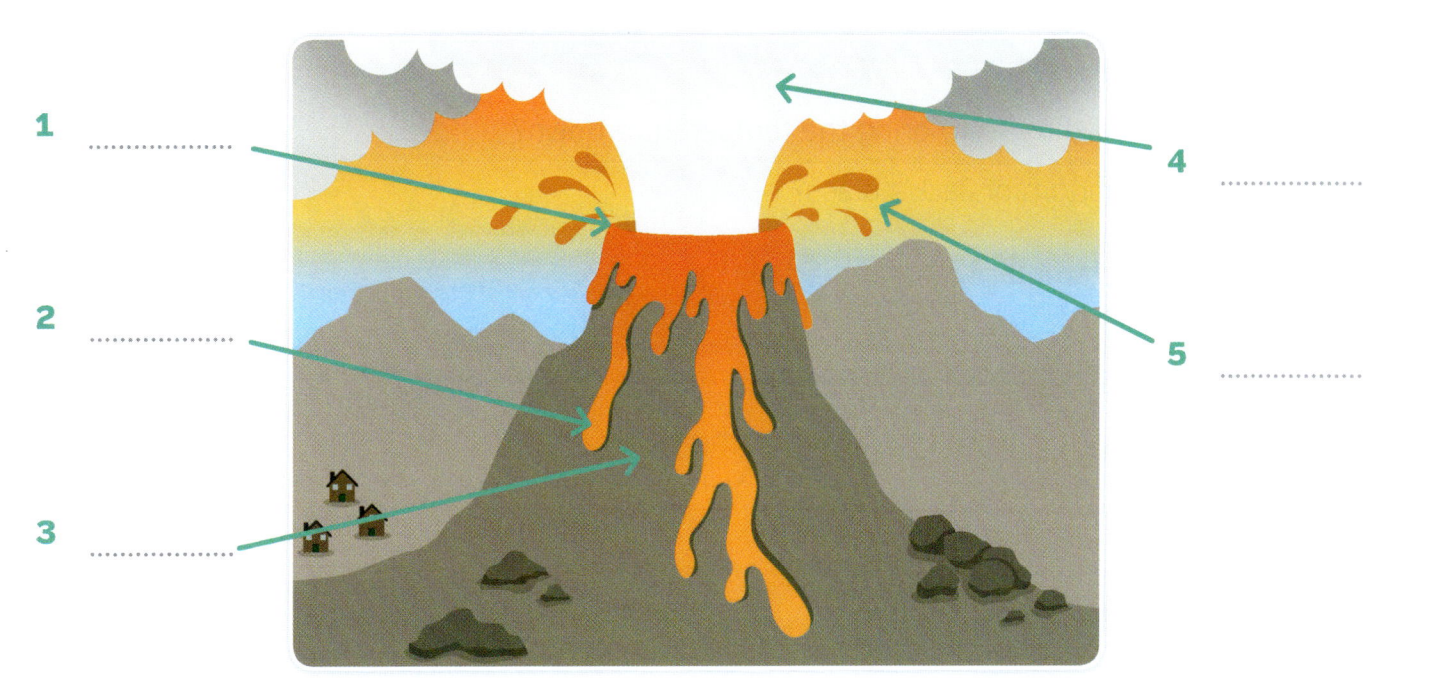

1 ....
2 ....
3 ....
4 ....
5 ....

3 Find words in *The Medallion Movers* that have the same meaning.

1 a piece of jewelry ....
2 the opposite of dangerous ....
3 fall down ....
4 moved quickly ....
5 movement of the ground ....
6 when you are in an unsafe situation ....
7 this is in the air after a volcano erupts ....

4 Think about the changes in the story at the end. Can you think of an alternative ending? Make notes and discuss with a friend.

Grammar 2

1 Watch Parts 2 and 3 of the story video. Answer the questions. Then read and complete.

> Be careful Jack. Don't fall over!

> We .... drop it!

1. What do they have to do to bring the temperature down?
2. What's on the bottom of Jack's glass?

2 Look at the grammar box and read.

Grammar

It's your decision. You **don't have to** go to the party.
At the weekend, I **don't have to** go to school!

You **mustn't** run across the street.
We **mustn't** shout in class.

Mustn't means prohibition and **don't have to** is just lack of obligation.

3 Read *The Medallion Movers* again and circle examples of *mustn't* and *don't have to*.

4 Read and complete. Use *mustn't* or *don't have to*.

1. You .... speak to the bus driver when the bus is moving.
2. It's a good idea to study for your exams, but you ....
3. We .... do our homework now, we can finish it later.
4. People .... talk loudly in the library.

5 Read and complete. Use *don't/doesn't have to* or *mustn't* and the words from the box.

> clean   get up   go   stay   study

Today's Sunday and Gale's in bed reading a book. She ¹ _____ early because there's no school. She ² _____ her room because she did that on Friday. She ³ _____ because there are no exams tomorrow. She's going to the swimming pool with her friends later but they ⁴ _____ before 3 p.m. because it's too hot. And they ⁵ _____ in the sun for a long time.

6 Think about the things you have to do at school. Make a list and compare with a friend.

Speaking 2

Speaking strategy

Be polite.

7 Look and discuss with a friend about what people have to do and don't have to do on each day.

WEATHER ALERT!

Monday	Tuesday	Wednesday	Thursday	Friday	Saturday	Sunday
sunny	rainy	cloudy	very sunny	snowy	windy	stormy

We don't have to wear a scarf and gloves on Monday.

Yes, you're right, but we mustn't go out without sunblock on Thursday! It's going to be really sunny!

Writing

1 Scan the text. Answer the questions.

1. Is the text telling a story or giving information about a journey?
2. What kind of text is it?

2 Read the text. Check your answers from Activity 1.

The Travel Planner
Desert Adventure

Episode 1
This week's journey starts at four o'clock in the morning. The team is in the Sahara Desert and they must travel across the desert, and survive! The extreme heat is dangerous and they need to be careful. They must drink enough water and take a lot of food for their journey. They're going to have to work hard, work together, and rest when they need to. Will they arrive at the next camp before it's dark and night time? **You mustn't miss it!**

3 Read the text again and circle any information you think is important.

4 **WB 85** Write a title for your new episode. Then go to the Workbook to do the writing activity.

Writing strategy

Before writing, find information on the Internet or in books, and think of the main points of the episode you want to include in your summary.

Now I Know

1 What happens in extreme conditions? Make notes about:

1 Extreme cold and hot temperatures.
2 Other examples of extreme conditions and weather.
3 Where we can find these conditions.
4 How extreme conditions can affect people.

2 Choose a project.

Prepare a Weather report

1 Work in groups and imagine an extreme weather situation.
2 One person is the weather forecaster. He/she will explain what happened and where.
3 The other group members are the reporters from different parts of the city. Explain what people are doing and what they have to do to stay safe.

or

How to stay safe

1 Choose an example of extreme conditions in a particular place or country. Find out about this place and the possible dangers.
2 Find or draw pictures that show the place and the dangers.
3 Write notes to tell people how to stay safe in these conditions.
4 Put your pictures and notes onto a poster and show it to the class.

Read and circle for yourself.

I can identify key points in facts and extract information about past events.

I can express my opinion.

I can identify the structure of texts. I can make basic inferences.

I can describe the plot of a movie or book.

99

7

How and why do fashions change?

Listening
- I can identify key details in factual talks.
- I can understand people's preferences.

Reading
- I can draw simple conclusions.
- I can predict what I think will happen next.

Speaking
- I can talk about an event in the past.
- I can make suggestions about activities.

Writing
- I can use appropriate greetings and closings in an email.

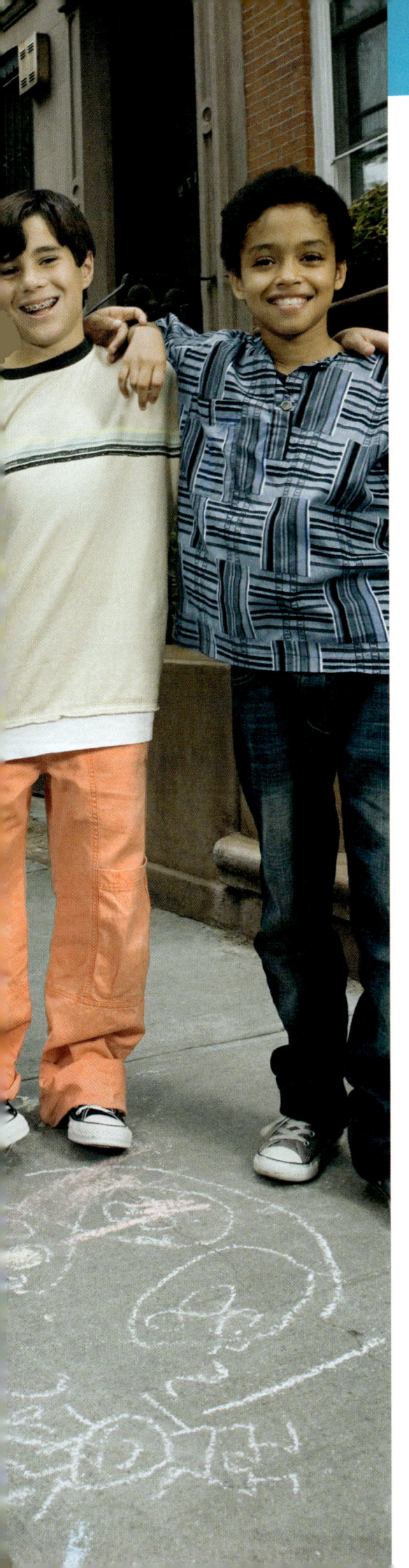

1 Look at the picture and discuss.

1 What clothes can you see in the picture?
2 What are the clothes made of?
3 What are your favorite clothes? Why?

2 Read and make notes. Then compare your answers with a friend.

1 Why do we wear different clothes?
2 Do you wear similar clothes to your parents?

3 Watch the video and answer the questions.

1 Where's the capital of the British fashion industry?
2 Why does Dylan want to be a fashion designer? And Izzy?
3 Have they designed clothes before?
4 What are Giles Deacon's top tips for a fashion designer?
5 What do most people working in fashion design start out as?

Pre-reading 1

1 💬 Discuss with a friend.

1. What kind of clothes do we wear now?
2. What kind of clothes did people wear in the past?

> **Reading strategy**
>
> Use information gained from pictures and words to understand the text.

2 💡 Read and answer. What do you think the website is for?

> Extravagant hats were very popular in the fifteenth century. Women's hats were often tall with long silk fabric on them. Men could choose from a wide variety of wool or felt hats. Women's dresses and men's cloaks were very long and they were made of wool. Blue was a new color to Europe and it was very fashionable.

3 🎧 2-07 Read *The Fashion Museum*. Find out about the exhibition.

Reading 1

The Fashion Museum
100 YEARS OF FASHION!

Exhibit dates:
MAY 20 – AUGUST 20

Book online

Tickets $10

Come and see our fantastic exhibit about fashion in the twentieth century. Learn about different fabrics. Find out what clothes people wore in each decade, from the 1900s to the 1990s.

[Image labels: collar, ribbon, vest]

1900s

In the 1900s, at the beginning of the twentieth century, people wore formal clothes. Women wore long dresses or long skirts, and blouses with high **collars**. They also wore hats with ribbons and feathers or flowers on them. Men wore three-piece suits – pants, a shirt, a **vest**, and a jacket. Clothes at this time were made of natural fibers, like silk, cotton, or **wool**. There were no clothes especially for children or young people.

1930s and 1940s

When the Second World War started, there wasn't much fabric to make clothes. So clothes became simpler and more practical. Men mostly wore army uniforms and women wore knee-length skirts with simple shirts and jackets. Before the war women didn't wear pants, but when the war started many women went to work and wore work pants for the first time.

They were usually made of **cotton**, wool, or denim. Some natural fabrics, like **silk**, became very expensive at this time and people started using **artificial fibers**, like nylon, to make clothes.

1960s and 1970s

In the 1960s and 1970s, fashions changed again. People had even more money and teenagers bought more clothes. Girls' skirts and dresses were shorter and more colorful than before. They were called mini-skirts or mini-dresses, and girls wore them with **patterned tights.** Boys wore shirts with colorful patterns or **suits** with tight pants.

Later in the 1970s people wore very wide pants called bell-bottoms and brightly-colored shirts with really big collars.

1950s

People started to wear more casual clothes after the war ended. They had more money to spend and for the first time there were clothes especially made for young people and teenagers. Girls liked to wear really wide skirts called poodle skirts, with blouses and short **cardigans**. These skirts were good for dancing rock and roll. Boys started to wear T-shirts, **leather** jackets, and blue jeans made of **denim**. Some boys, called Teddy Boys, wore colorful tight pants and long jackets.

1980s

At the end of the twentieth century, comfortable sports clothes became more popular with both boys and girls. Girls often wore tights or leggings made of artificial fibers like lycra. They wore them with wool leg warmers and very big sweaters. Boys wore sweatpants and sweatshirts with patterns and sports shoes. Denim jeans and denim jackets were also very fashionable and popular.

Today our clothes are influenced by all the fashions from the twentieth century. Which is your favorite?

4 Which of the fashions do you like best? Why do you think fashions changed during the twentieth century? How are they different from today's fashions?

Comprehension 1

1 Read *The Fashion Museum* again and answer.

1. What's the website for?
2. What's the name of the exhibit?
3. How much are the tickets?
4. Would you like to visit the exhibit? Why?

2 Read and circle.

1. In the 1900s, clothes were made of **natural** / **artificial** fibers.
2. In the 1940s, women wore **jackets** / **pants** for the first time.
3. Clothes especially for young people were first made in the **1900s** / **1950s**.
4. In the 1960s, skirts were **longer** / **shorter** than before.
5. Clothes in the 1960s and 1970s were **colorful** / **dark**.

3 Match the clothes to each decade.

1900s   1940s   1950s   1960s   1980s

- blue jeans
- leather jackets

- mini-skirts
- patterned tights

- big sweaters
- sports clothes

- uniforms
- work pants

- long dresses
- high collars

Listening 1

4 What fabrics can you name? What do you know about them?

Listening strategy
Listen for details.

5 (2-08) Listen to the quiz. What fabric words do you hear?

6 (2-09) Listen again and match.

1. Cotton comes from
2. Denim pants were first made by
3. Silk comes from a
4. Leather is made from
5. Nylon is used to make
6. Lycra is an artificial fabric that is

a. Levi Strauss.
b. silkworm.
c. stretchy.
d. a plant.
e. animal skin.
f. women's tights.

7 Why do you think we use different fabrics to make clothes? Have you seen any clothes made of unusual fabrics? Discuss with a friend.

104

Vocabulary 1

1 Find these words in *The Fashion Museum*. Circle the words for fabrics and underline the words for clothes.

> artificial fibers   cardigan   collar   cotton   denim   leather
> pattern   tights   silk   suit   vest   wool

2 🎧 2-10 Listen and say. Use the words from Activity 1.

3 Read and circle.

1. My mom's blouse has a high **collar** / **fabric**.
2. My dad wears formal clothes to work. He wears a **cardigan** / **suit**.
3. My grandpa wears a shirt under his **vest** / **T-shirt**.
4. To keep my legs warm in the winter, I wear wool **sweaters** / **tights**.
5. I like colorful clothes made from natural fibers, such as **nylon** / **cotton**.

4 💬 Write two kinds of clothes made of each fiber. Compare with a friend.

Artificial fibers	Cotton	Silk

Leather	Wool	Denim

5 💬 What clothes do you have that are made of natural fibers or artificial fibers? Which do you prefer? Why? Discuss with a friend.

105

Grammar 1

1 Watch Part 1 of the story video. Where do they go? Then number the sentences in order.

The Doctor and his friends saw the man when they arrived at the museum.

.... They ran to the wax museum.
.... They traveled to London in the TARDIS.
.... They followed the man inside.
.... They saw a garbage truck dropping trash.

2 Read the grammar box and match.

> **Grammar**
>
> I had breakfast **before** I went to school.
> I went to school **after** I had breakfast.
> I had classes **when** I got to school.
>
> 1 They got into the TARDIS a when they arrived at the museum.
> 2 They ran to the wax museum b before they traveled to London.
> 3 They saw the man c after they saw the garbage truck.

3 Read *The Fashion Museum* again and circle examples of *before*, *after*, and *when*.

4 What did you do yesterday? Complete the sentences with *before*, *after*, or *when*.

1. I got dressed .... I went to school.
2. I brushed my teeth .... I had breakfast.
3. I watched TV .... I had dinner.
4. I took a bath .... I went to bed.
5. I played soccer .... I got to my friend's house.

5 Look at Marc's diary. Write sentences with *before*, *after*, and *when*.

Time	Activity
8:00 a.m.	woke up
8:15 a.m.	got dressed
8:30 a.m.	had breakfast
9:00 a.m.	got to Sam's house, had a snack
11:00 a.m.	played video games
12:00 p.m.	had lunch
2:00 p.m.	played soccer
4:00 p.m.	went to the swimming pool
6:00 p.m.	had dinner
7:00 p.m.	had dessert, watched TV
9:00 p.m.	went to bed, fell asleep

1. *Marc got dressed after he woke up.*
2. *He had a snack when ...*
3. ....
4. ....
5. ....
6. ....

Speaking 1

6 💬 What did you do yesterday? Complete the diary. Then discuss with a friend. Use *before*, *after,* and *when*.

Speaking strategy
Use key grammar words to ask questions.

Time	Activity

What did you do yesterday evening?

I had dinner early. I had dinner before I watched TV.

Pre-reading 2

1 Are there any old clothes or objects in your house? Who do/did they belong to? Discuss with a friend.

> **Reading strategy**
>
> Think about and recount a story.

2 Read and answer. What do you think the children will find in the cellar? What do you think will happen in the story?

Iris, Felix and Stefan were at their grandma's house for the weekend. Grandma fell asleep after dinner.

"I'm bored!" said Felix.
"What shall we do?"
"I know! Let's explore!"
"Great idea!" said Iris.
"There's a door that Grandma always keeps closed. I think it goes down into the cellar! Why don't we go down there and see what we can find?"

---

3 🎧 2-11 Read *The Treasure in the Attic*. Find out about the treasure the children find.

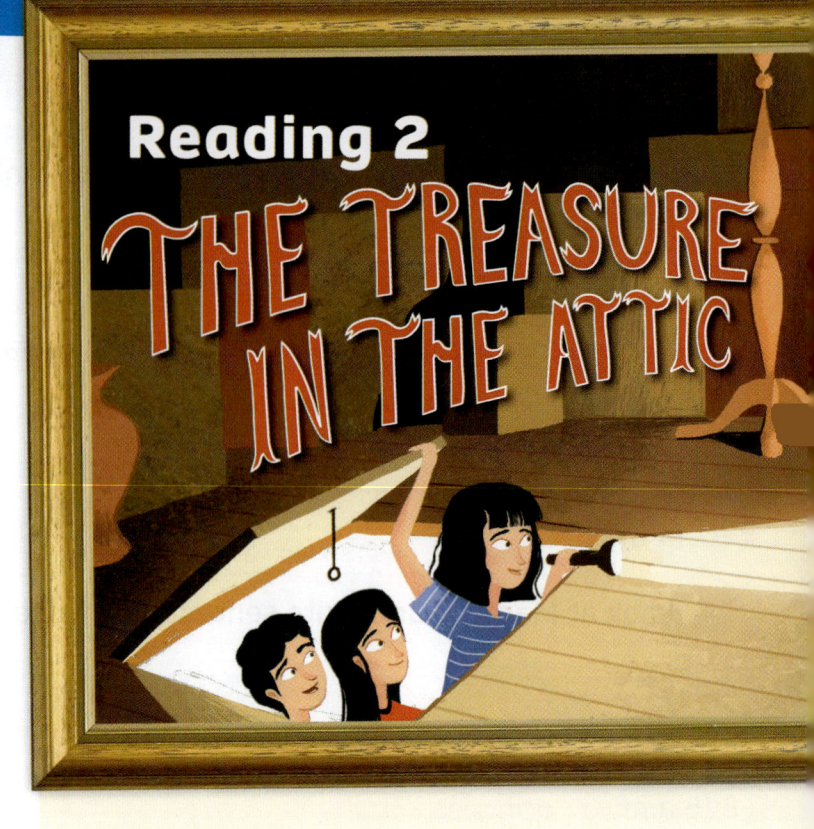

Reading 2
THE TREASURE IN THE ATTIC

Maia, Jaime and Saira were at home one rainy day.

"I'm bored!" said Jaime. "What shall we do?"

"I know! Why don't we **dress up**?" suggested Maia. "There are some dressing-up clothes upstairs. We could dress up as pirates! Arr!"

"That's a great idea!" said Saira.

The children went upstairs to find the dressing-up box. When they were there, Saira noticed a ladder. It went up to a trapdoor in the ceiling.

"What's up there?" she asked.

"Oh, that's just the attic," answered Maia.

"Shall we go up and explore?" suggested Saira.

"Yes, let's explore!" said Jaime.

"I don't think that's a good idea. Mum doesn't like us to go up there," said Maia.

"Oh, come on! We could just have a quick look!" said Saira.

"Oh, OK!" agreed Maia. The children climbed slowly up the ladder and opened the trapdoor.

"It's dark in here. I can't see!" complained Maia.

"We could **borrow** Dad's torch! I'll go and get it!" said Jaime.

Jaime found the torch and shone it into the attic. They saw a big, old, wooden box in the middle of the room.

"What's in the box? Let's look inside!" said Saira.

The children opened the heavy lid of the box. Inside there was another smaller box. When they opened the smaller box, they saw something sparkling in the light.

"Wow! Look at this! It's an old **necklace**! It's beautiful!" said Saira.

"Yes, it is, but it looks very **delicate**. Be careful! It might break," said Maia.

"There are some **earrings** and a **bracelet** here too! They're very old!" said Saira.

"And there's an old pocket **watch** too! And a **ribbon** … with a medal on it! How cool!" said Jaime.

"Look, there's an old picture too. The lady's wearing a beautiful silk dress! And the man's wearing a uniform with a big leather **belt**. Who are they?" asked Saira.

Suddenly, the children heard footsteps on the stairs. They stopped talking.

"We should hide!" whispered Jaime.

Then they heard a familiar voice, "Maia? Jaime? What are you doing up there?" asked Mum, as she climbed up into the attic.

"Oh, we were just exploring, and we found this box … " said Jaime.

"What are these things in the box, Mum?" asked Maia.

"Oh! I forgot that box was up here! That's a picture of your great-grandmother and your great-grandfather on their wedding day!" said Mum. "And this is the **jewellery** your great-grandmother wore that day! It was **designed** by a famous jewellery designer."

"Wow!" exclaimed Maia.

"And is this Great-grandfather's medal?" asked Jaime.

"Yes, it is! He was very brave in the war!" said Mum.

"So you aren't cross with us for coming up here?" asked Jaime.

"No! It's lucky you did. Now we have these lovely things to look at and we can remember your great-grandparents!" said Mum happily.

4 Do you have any special things at home that belonged to members of your family in the past? Would you use them today? Why?/Why not?

Comprehension 2

1 Read *The Treasure in the Attic* again and answer.

1 Why did the children go into the attic?
2 What did they find there?
3 Who did the things in the box belong to?
4 How do you think they felt when they found the box?

2 Read and write **T** (true) or **F** (false).

1 The children decided to dress up. ....
2 They went upstairs because they wanted to find some jewelry. ....
3 Saira suggested going up into the attic. ....
4 Jaime used his own flashlight to light up the attic. ....
5 The box in the attic was full of dressing-up clothes. ....
6 Mom was happy when she saw the box in the attic. ....

3 Read and match.

1	to dress up	a	something that isn't very strong
2	to borrow	b	a room at the top of a house
		c	something you use to tell the time
3	jewelry		
		d	to use somebody else's things for a short time
4	attic		
		e	to put on clothes to play a children's game
5	delicate		
		f	pretty things worn on the neck, ears, hands, and arms
6	watch		

Listening 2

Listening strategy

Listen for suggestions.

4 🎧 2-12 Listen to the conversation. What are the children talking about?

5 🎧 2-13 Look at the plan of the museum. Listen again and check (✓) the places they decide to visit.

LIVING HISTORY MUSEUM

General store
Old schoolhouse
Fairground
Tram station
Clothes collection
Old candy store
Picnic area

6 💬 Imagine you're at the Living History Museum. Discuss with a friend. Make suggestions about where to go.

Vocabulary 2

1 Find these words in *The Treasure in the Attic*. Which words are things that you can wear?

> belt   borrow   bracelet
> delicate   design   dress up
> earrings   jewelry   necklace
> ribbon   watch

2 🎧 2-14 Listen and say. Use the words from Activity 1.

3 Read, choose, and write.

> bracelet   earrings   jewelry
> necklace   ribbons   watch

Maria: Look at these beautiful things in Mom's ¹_____ box! They're so sparkly!

Ana: Let's try them on!

Maria: Yes, good idea! Look at this ²_____. It looks so nice around my neck. But the ³_____ is too big for my wrist.

Ana: These ⁴_____ look really nice in my ears!

Maria: I love Mom's ⁵_____. It tells the time and looks pretty, too.

Ana: And I like the ⁶_____ she uses to tie up her hair. Mom has some really nice things!

4 Read and circle.

1 I don't have my watch with me. Could I **borrow** / **break** / **buy** yours?

2 Mom's necklace is pretty, but it's easy to break. It's **strong** / **expensive** / **delicate**.

3 My little sister likes to wear a princess costume. She likes to dress **up** / **on** / **in**.

4 I want to learn how to **discover** / **digest** / **design** clothes.

5 Earrings, necklaces, and bracelets are all kinds of **sculpture** / **jewelry** / **plastic**.

5 💬 Discuss with a friend.

1 Do you like dressing up? What's your favorite costume?

2 When did you last borrow something? What was it? Who did you borrow it from?

3 Do you have any jewelry? Do you have a watch? Can you describe it?

> I love dressing up as a superhero!

> I borrowed my sister's hair ribbon last week.

Grammar 2

1 🎬 7-3 BBC Watch Part 2 of the story video. Then read and complete.

> I know! .... turn on the lights!

2 🎬 7-4 BBC Watch Parts 2 and 3 of the story video. Then answer the questions.

1 Who's the Doctor looking for in the wax museum?
2 What's the king wearing?
3 Who's controlling the king?

3 Read the grammar box and complete.

4 Read *The Treasure in the Attic* again and circle phrases that the children use to suggest ideas.

Grammar

Let's turn off the lights!
We **should/could** turn off the lights!

Shall I/we turn off the lights?
Should I/we turn off the lights?
Why don't you/we turn off the lights?

1 The Smogator is coming! We .... hide!
2 .... we run this way?
3 .... change our clothes!
4 .... I use the Smogsucker?

5 Write the words in the correct order.

1 we / swimming / go / shall
....?

2 don't / why / we / shopping / go
....?

3 go / the / museum / let's / to / fashion
....!

4 should / wear / we / our / sneakers
....

6 Read and complete. Use the words and phrases from the grammar box.

1
What shall we do today?

.... go to the sports center?

Yes, that's a good idea. We .... play basketball!

Great! .... go!

2
.... visit the Fashion Museum today?

That's not a bad idea! .... we have lunch before we go?

OK. .... have pizza?

No! .... have burgers!

Speaking 2

7 Think about the activities below. Discuss with your group. Make a plan for a day out.

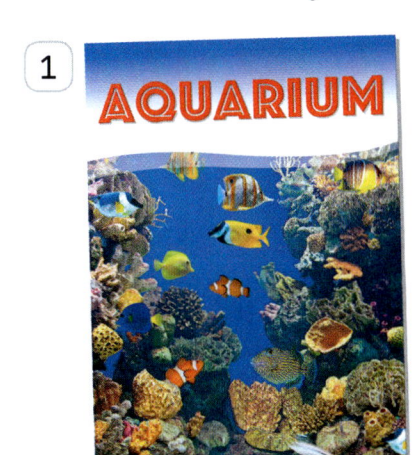

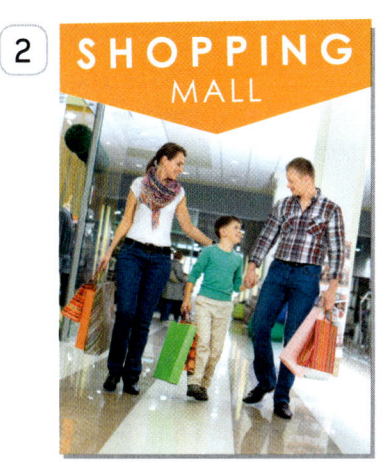

1 AQUARIUM
2 SHOPPING MALL
3 PIZZA

Why don't we go to the aquarium first?

Yes, that's a good idea. We could see some fish!

After that, let's have pizza for lunch!

No, we should have sushi. It's healthier!

Then after lunch, we could go to the shopping mall!

Writing

1 Scan the texts. Answer the questions.

1. What kind of texts are they?
2. Who's writing the texts?
3. What's the purpose of the texts?

To: Alex - alex@email.com
From: Laila - laila@home.com
Subject: School disco

Hello Alex,

I didn't see you after school, so just wanted to ask you about the disco tomorrow. What are you going to wear? I think I'm going to wear my jeans and my new cardigan. You know, the one with the red and white patterns. I can't decide whether to wear my black or blue jeans. Why don't you come to my house before we go? Then we can decide what to wear and get ready together.

My parents said they can take us to the disco if you want.

Love,

Laila

To: Laila - laila@home.com
From: Alex - alex@email.com
Subject: RE: School disco

Hi Laila,

Yes, good idea! That would be awesome! I think I'm going to wear my denim jacket and my blue T-shirt. Why don't we wear our new sneakers, too? They're good for dancing! I'll come home with you from school and then we can get ready! I can't wait for the disco, it's going to be so cool!

See you tomorrow,

Alex

---

2 Read the texts. Check your answers from Activity 1.

3 Circle the correct informal greetings and closing phrases.

1. Dear Isabella / Hi Isabella
2. Love / Best wishes
3. Hi Alex / Dear Alex
4. Yours sincerely / See you tomorrow

4 **WB 99** Find or draw pictures of your weekend. Then go to the Workbook to do the writing activity.

Writing strategy

Use appropriate informal greetings and closing phrases in an email.

Hello, *Hi*, *Love*, *See you soon*.

Now I Know

1 How and why do fashions change? Look back through Unit 7. Use the information you learned to answer the questions. Add your own ideas.

1. Why are people interested in fashion?
   ....
2. Why do we wear different kinds of clothes?
   ....
3. Why do we use different fabrics to make clothes?
   ....
4. Why do fashions change?
   ....

2 Choose a project.

Work in a small group. Role-play a clothes shopping trip.

1. Decide why you want to buy some new clothes, e.g. for a party.
2. In your group, make and respond to suggestions about what to buy.
3. Record your dialog by writing it down or making an audio recording.
4. Role-play your dialog for the class.

or

Design some clothes for a special occasion.

1. Choose an occasion.
2. Decide what kind of clothes you're going to design for the occasion.
3. Choose the fabrics for your clothes.
4. Draw and label the clothes.
5. Present them to the class. Explain your choices.

Read and circle for yourself.

I can identify key details in factual talks.
I can understand people's preferences.

I can talk about an event in the past.
I can make suggestions about activities.

I can draw simple conclusions. I can predict what I think will happen next.

I can use appropriate greetings and closings in an email.

8

How has entertainment developed?

Listening
- I can understand details in dialogs.
- I can understand someone's reasons.

Reading
- I can identify key words and phrases.
- I can identify the writer's overall purpose.

Speaking
- I can make suggestions about what to do.
- I can talk about plans for the near furture.

Writing
- I can give my opinion on a familiar topic.

1 Look at the picture and discuss.

1. What can you see in the picture?
2. What kind of dance do you think it is? Is it modern or traditional?
3. Why do you think they're dancing?

2 Read and make notes. Then compare your answers with a friend.

1. Imagine you have an audition for a performance. How do you prepare for an audition? How would you feel?
2. Have you ever been in a performance? What was the performance? What was your role in the performance? Did you enjoy it?

3 Watch the video. Then write T (true) or F (false).

1. Adam is an art teacher. ....
2. When creating animations, it's important to draw out the different stages of your animation first. ....
3. Once you record your voices, it's important to save the recording. ....
4. Make sure you post your animation online before you make any final edits to it. ....

117

Pre-reading 1

1 💬 Discuss with a friend.

1. Are music and dancing important to you? Why?
2. Do you dance when you listen to your favorite music? Why?/Why not?
3. How do you feel when you listen to music or dance?

> **📖 Reading strategy**
>
> Choose the most important information to summarize what you're reading.

2 💡 Read and answer. Can you summarize what the text is about in one sentence?

> This week we're looking at hoop dancing. You can probably twirl a hoop around your waist, arms or legs, but can you do it to music? We can see traditional hoop dancing in some Native American tribes, and you might also see hoop dancing performances in rhythmic gymnastics. There are even exercise classes using hoops. They're a bit heavier, but it looks good fun!

3 🎧 2-15 Read *Winning Combinations!*. How has dance developed from prehistoric times?

Reading 1

WINNING COMBINATIONS!

Dance and music are an important part of our lives today, and they were important many years ago too. We know that dance goes back in history to prehistoric times. We can see this in cave paintings from as far back as 9,000 years ago!

Music and dance were part of many old traditions, and were a form of entertainment for their **audiences**. Watching different dance **performances** can be breathtaking! Some of these traditions still exist today, and others are developing into more modern music and styles of dancing.

Traditional and classical dances have got different styles. The style depends on the country and culture the dance is from. Other classical dances are hundreds of years old and started in one country, but are now danced all over the world – like **ballroom dancing**.

There are several kinds of dance people learn when they start ballroom dancing. A few, for example, are the **waltz** (which started in Germany in the eighteenth century), the **tango** (which dates back to the late 1800s in Argentina), the **samba** (is more recent and dates to the beginning of the twentieth century in Brazil) and the **jive** (which began in the United States in the 1930s). These are a few examples, and recognising the different dances can be difficult, but even harder to dance them!

In traditional and classical dance, there are particular steps, movements and **rhythms**. Some kinds of dances are individual, friend dances, or in small or large groups. **Ballet** is an example of a classical dance. It's usually easy to recognise because a lot of dancers are "en pointe." This refers to the pointe shoes they wear, so they look like they're dancing on the tips of their toes.

Ballet goes back to the fifteenth century. It began in Italy, but ballet "en pointe" didn't start until the late nineteenth century. Today, we can see classical ballet and contemporary ballet. Contemporary ballet uses classical ballet with more modern dances. Some dance schools and companies use ballet techniques with modern music like jazz or **rock** and **hip-hop**!

What about mixing ballet and hip-hop? Can you mix hip-hop and ballet dancing? Yes, you can, and it's called hiplet™. It's a new contemporary dance style. **Hiplet™** dancers are classically trained in ballet and learn to dance "en pointe." They combine movements of classical ballet with movements and music from hip-hop. It's a very new style, but its popularity is growing.

So, we all move to a beat. We all enjoy moving to music we like. Some songs get us tapping our feet or moving our whole bodies. How about the bachata from the Dominican Republic and the Argentine tango? Check out next week's column on bachatango! Will it be a winning combination for you?

4 Do you think you would prefer to watch a classical or contemporary dance performance? Why?

Comprehension 1

1 Read *Winning Combinations!* again. Which two sentences best summarize the text?

a   Dance and music are recent and modern inventions.
b   In the past, dance was used for entertainment.
c   Dance has changed a lot over the years.
d   Some kinds of dance are more difficult than others.
e   There are new styles of some classical dances.

2 Read and circle.

1   We know that dance was important in prehistoric times because **it was a tradition** / **we can see dance in cave paintings**.
2   In ballroom dancing, there are **several dances** / **two dances**.
3   Traditional ballet started in **France** / **Italy**.
4   Ballet "en pointe" **began in** / **developed after** the fifteenth century.
5   Hiplet™ is a combination of ballet and **jive** / **hip-hop**.
6   Bachata is a dance from **the Dominican Republic** / **Argentina**.

3 Match each dance to a date and location.

Waltz	Argentina	1930s
Ballet	Germany	18th century
Jive	Brazil	20th century
Samba	United States	1800s
Tango	Italy	15th century

120

Listening 1

4 What kind of entertainment or performance do you sometimes see in public places?

> **Listening strategy**
>
> Listen for the details given to answer specific questions.

5 2-16 Listen to the interview. What kind of performance do they discuss?

6 2-17 Listen again and write **T** (true) or **F** (false).

1   Alisha was in the supermarket. ......
2   There were less than 30 people watching the performance. ......
3   A flashmob is a group of people dancing. ......
4   A flashmob only performs in a theater. ......
5   People are waiting and expecting to see a performance. ......
6   The group might dance something modern. ......

7 Have you ever seen a flashmob? Would you like to take part in one?

Vocabulary 1

1 Find these words in *Winning Combinations!*. Which words describe a kind of dance?

> audience   ballet   ballroom dancing   hip-hop   hiplet™   jive
> performance   rhythm   rock   samba   tango   waltz

2 Complete the chart. Use words from Activity 1.

Classical dance	Modern dance	Combination dance	Other dance/music words

3 Write two examples for each heading. Then compare with a friend.

Places you might find an audience
....
....

Other modern dances
....
....

BALLROOM DANCES
....
....

Kinds of performance
....
....

4 Read the questions.

1 Would you like to be a professional dancer? Why?/Why not?
2 Can you name any movies about dancing?
3 Which do you prefer – watching movies about dancing or music performances? Why?

Grammar 1

1 Watch Part 1 of the story video. What does Kim want to do? Then read and complete.

What do you _____?
How about _____ tonight?

2 Read the grammar box and circle.

> **Grammar**
>
> **What about** going to a concert tonight? Yes, let's do that!
> **How about** eating some pizza for dinner? That's a great idea!
>
> 1 How about **buy** / **buying** some fruit for lunch? Good idea.
> 2 What about **playing** / **play** tennis on Saturday? Great! At what time?

3 Read *Winning Combinations!* again. Circle examples of *what about* and *how about*.

4 Read and match. Then complete the suggestions.

1 I'm hungry.
2 We're bored.
3 You're too busy now.
4 Dad doesn't like driving.
5 My homework is difficult.

a How about asking _____ for some help?
b What about taking a _____ to get there?
c What about watching a _____ ? That's fun!
d How about making a _____ to eat?
e How about going to _____ when you're finished?

122

> The concert **is starting** at eight o'clock.
> My sister **is performing** in a show on Sunday.
> I **am meeting** my friend outside the arts center.
> **Are** you **meeting** your grandparents on Sunday?

5 Complete the sentences. Use the correct form of the verbs in parentheses.

1. We _____ (watch) the ballet performance on Saturday at 7:00 p.m.
2. The movie _____ (show) at 6:00 p.m.
3. My sister _____ (perform) in her street dance show on Friday.
4. _____ you _____ (meet) before the movie to buy popcorn?
5. The party is _____ (start) at 6.30 p.m. on Saturday.
6. Are you _____ (meet) me before Coding Club?
7. My brother _____ (play) soccer on Saturday.

Speaking 1

6 Look at the events. Then discuss with your friends.

Speaking strategy

Give reasons to explain your answer.

Friday
Hip-hop show 4:00 p.m.
Pop concert 7:00 p.m.

Saturday
Samba class 6:00 p.m.
Ballet performance 7:00 p.m.

Sunday
Family lunch 12:30 p.m.
New movie 7:30 p.m.

- What are you doing on Saturday?
- What about going to a pop concert after?
- My sister is performing in a hip-hop show.

Pre-reading 2

1 💬 Discuss with a friend.

1 What kind of movies do you like watching?
2 What's your favorite movie and why do you like it?

> **Reading strategy**
>
> Identify reasons why certain details are given in a story.

2 💡 Read and answer. Why do you think we're told about the school classes Carlos has?

Carlos got up early. He got dressed and put his books in his backpack. He had drama, English, P.E., and history on Mondays. He loved English and writing stories, and he loved drama, but he really enjoyed the things that combined the two. Carlos wanted to be a writer and a director.

"I'll go to London and I'll be famous when I'm older," Carlos dreamed.

"Carlos! Hurry up! You don't want to be late for school!" his mom shouted from downstairs.

3 🎧 2-18 Read *Movie Stars in the Making*. Why do you think Kim's mom sends Charlotte and Eleanor into the play room?

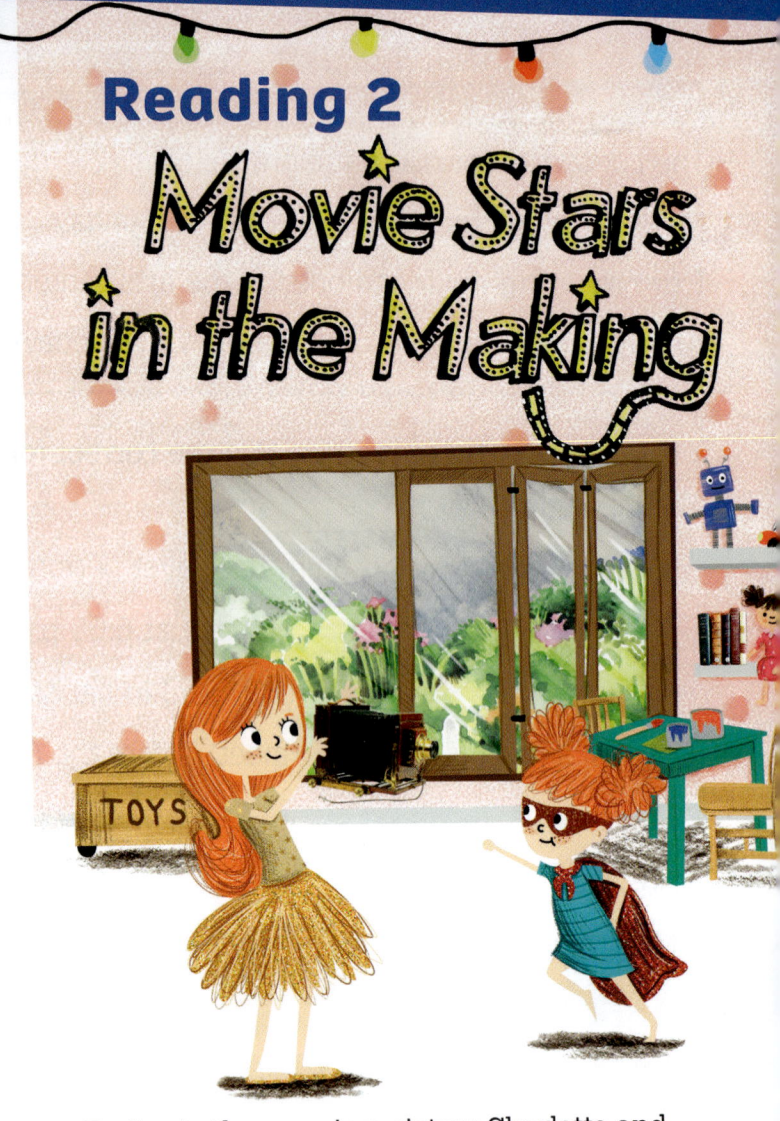

Reading 2

Movie Stars in the Making

Earlier in the morning, sisters Charlotte and Eleanor visited their cousin Kim. They always visited on a Saturday to watch their favorite **reality TV** show, but she wasn't at home today. "I'll call your uncle and see where they are – they just popped out. They're visiting your grandparents," said Auntie Julia. "Do you want to go through to the play room, girls? I'm sure they won't be long. I'll bring you a drink in a minute."

Charlotte and Eleanor went through to the play room. Charlotte noticed a piece of paper and a notebook on the table. "It's from Kim. It says, *The Charlotte and Eleanor Show!* I'll read it." Eleanor nodded her head enthusiastically.

They sat and read the notebook. They laughed. They laughed so hard their tummies hurt. It had everything, from **horror**, to **action**, to **comedy**, to **drama**, and even to **animation**. Kim was a very talented writer.

"OK, let's follow her instructions ... but where's the camera?" Charlotte shrugged her shoulders.
"Is that it over there?" said Eleanor pointing across the room.
Charlotte frowned. "It looks so old, where did she find this?! It must be vintage. Do you think it'll even work?"
"There's only one way to find out!" squeaked Eleanor as she skipped across the room and grabbed it.

Auntie Julia popped her head around the door. "Is everything OK, girls? Uncle Tom and Kim are stuck in traffic. They'll be back later."
"Yeah, we're fine," said the girls. They were so excited and busy that they didn't really notice Auntie Julia with their drinks.

They lost track of time and followed all of Kim's instructions ... and **lines**. There were so many lines, but they loved learning lines for things like their school **plays** and could remember them very quickly. They took turns being the **director**, but were also both in front of the camera. They used everything in the dressing-up box, including the **make-up**. Hours went by and finally they finished. "THE END!" they laughed, and fell onto the couch.

"Are you hungry, girls?" shouted Auntie Julia. "I'm meeting a friend at Peppers and Pizzas in 30 minutes. Do you want to come?"
"Definitely!" Charlotte could hear her tummy rumbling.
"Perfect timing!" said Eleanor, running into the kitchen.

Later ...

The big, white sheet was hanging across the yard. This was going to be brilliant. Everywhere was dark, but the stars were sparkling in the sky. Everyone was sitting in the yard waiting. They all gave a big round of **applause** ... as Auntie Julia, Charlotte, and Eleanor walked into the yard.

Eleanor and Charlotte were totally surprised. "What's going on?" asked Eleanor, looking around at everyone sitting there. There was Mom and Dad, Grandpa and Grandma, Uncle Tom, and other friends and family.
"It's *The Charlotte and Eleanor Show!*" laughed Kim as she hugged Eleanor and Charlotte. "I can't wait to see the final show. When you went for pizza, I **edited** it. It's definitely a comedy!"
"We thought Auntie Julia ate her pizza slowly!" Charlotte laughed.

As they turned to look at Auntie Julia, they saw the show was projected onto the white sheet.
"Lights, camera, action!" said Kim waving everyone to sit down and watch.

4 Do you go to the movies often? Have you ever been to an open air showing of a movie? How else can you watch movies?

Comprehension 2

1 Read *Movie Stars in the Making* again and answer.

1 Do you think Kim and Uncle Tom were really stuck in traffic?
2 Why do you think Auntie Julia took the girls for pizza?

2 Read and circle. Then discuss with a friend and give reasons for your answers.

1 Charlotte and Eleanor **were / weren't** very surprised at the end of the story.
2 Charlotte and Eleanor **enjoyed / didn't enjoy** acting.
3 **Kim / Charlotte and Eleanor** planned the surprise.

3 Read and check (✓) the sentences you think are true.

1 Kim was sure Eleanor and Charlotte were going to follow her instructions. ☐
2 Auntie Julia didn't know where Kim was. ☐
3 Charlotte and Eleanor knew they were going to see their show later. ☐
4 The family wanted to surprise Charlotte and Eleanor. ☐
5 All of Charlotte and Eleanor's family and friends knew about the show. ☐
6 Kim likes to write and edit shows. ☐

Listening 2

4 What are your favorite video games and apps?

> **Listening strategy**
>
> Listen for the reasons people give about why they like or don't like something.

5 🎧 2-19 Listen to Bea and Chloe. What kinds of apps are they talking about? Check (✓).

sleep app ☐   photo app ☐
food app ☐   music app ☐
video editing app ☐ games apps ☐
dance steps app ☐

6 🎧 2-20 Listen again and complete.

1 Bea likes the video editing app because she can _____.
2 Chloe likes using photo apps because she thinks the _____ are funny.
3 Chloe doesn't like looking at a screen for too long because it isn't _____.
4 Chloe plays *Turtle Trails* because there's a new _____ each day.

7 Can you think of any other kinds of games? For example, are there any board games or mime games you enjoy? Discuss with a friend.

Vocabulary 2

1 Find these words in *Movie Stars in the Making*. What do you think they mean?

> action   animation   applause
> comedy   director   drama
> edit   horror   lines
> make-up   play   reality TV

2 Match the words from Activity 1 to the definitions.

1 This usually happens at the end of a good performance. ....

2 These movies are often fast and there might be explosions. ....

3 Sometimes these movies can be scary. ....

4 A kind of show about real people and their lives. They don't have lines to learn. ....

5 These kinds of movies make us laugh. ....

6 This happens to all of the video recordings to make a final movie. ....

7 This person is in charge of making a movie and directs the actors. ....

8 This kind of movie uses pictures, drawings, and people's voices. ....

9 Actors need to learn and remember these. ....

10 This is put on the face or body. ....

3 Which are your two favorite words from the word box? Choose and write sentences with them in your notebook.

4 🎧 2-21 Listen and number the movie ads in the order you hear them. Which movie would you like to see? Why?

drama ☐   horror ☐
action ☐   comedy ☐

5 Read the questions. Discuss with a friend.

1 Do you like watching reality TV?

2 Would you like to be on a reality TV show? Why?/Why not?

3 Do you think reality TV can have a negative impact on people?

127

Grammar 2

1 Watch Parts 2 and 3 of the story video. What do they do on stage? Then read and complete.

I'm going to _____ a concert tonight!

2 Read the grammar box and complete.

Grammar

I**'m meeting** my best friend after school.
My grandma **is visiting** us next week.
We use the Present Progressive to talk about definite future arrangements.

The concert starts at 1:00 p.m. I**'ll buy** the tickets online now.
Those bags are too heavy, Mom. I**'ll help** you.
We use *will* for spontaneous decisions.

Next week is a holiday and I ¹_____ (do) a lot of things! On Monday, I ²_____ (see) my friends and we ³_____ (go) to a concert. On Tuesday, I ⁴_____ (visit) my cousins. I ⁵_____ (call) them now and ask them if they want to go to a dance performance.

3 Read *Movie Stars in the Making* again and circle the spontaneous decisions and the definite arrangements Auntie Julia makes.

4 Read and check (✓) the sentences that describe planned events.

1 My family and I are traveling to Italy for a vacation. We have the tickets! ☐
2 What would you like to eat? Let me see … OK, I'll have the chicken with salad. ☐
3 It's getting dark. I'll turn on the lights. ☐
4 My mom is teaching me how to cook lunch tomorrow. We have all the ingredients. ☐

5 Read and complete. Use the *Present Progressive*, *will*, and the words in parentheses.

1 The show looks brilliant! I _____ (try) and book us a seat now.
2 I can't watch the movie with you tomorrow. We _____ (visit) the museum.
3 Yes, let's go. I _____ (call) the restaurant and tell them you're vegetarian.
4 I _____ (play) soccer later. Do you want to come?
5 They want to see the ballet tomorrow, but they _____ (study) for a school test.

Speaking 2

6 Imagine you're a dancer, musician, or singer in a band. Complete the chart. Then discuss with the band members about your arrangements for next week.

Band members	Planned	To do
Rob – singer	show – Monday	practice songs

We're playing at the Imperial Stadium next Monday.

Yes, and we're going to France on Tuesday. What about the train tickets?

Oh, yes, I forgot! I'll buy them now!

129

Writing

1 Scan the text. Answer the questions.

1 What's the purpose of the text?
   a to give information about a movie
   b to give information and an opinion about a movie
   c to give a story
2 Does it make you want to see the movie?

THE RETURN OF THE FAB FIVE

The Return of the Fab Five is a comedy about five superheroes. They have to save the planet from a terrible monster. The monster wants to turn children into robots and steal their imagination! The children lose their ability to play music and create stories, and their world becomes gray and boring.

The five superheroes devise a plan to capture the monster and give the children back their creativity.

The superheroes are active and fly everywhere. The movie is fast paced and dramatic and at last the superheroes rescue the children from the grayness of life without creativity.

The director and the actors did a great job. The story is exciting and there's an interesting mix of classical music, rap, and rock. You should see this movie! The movie opens at the Cinebox next Saturday.

2 Read the text. Check your answers from Activity 1.

3 Read the text again. Circle examples of descriptions and opinions.

4 **WB 113** Find or draw pictures of your favorite movie or show. Then go to the Workbook to do the writing activity.

Writing strategy

Use descriptions and your opinion to give a review.

... a comedy about five superheroes. The story is exciting ...

Now I Know

1 How has entertainment developed? Look back through Unit 8 and make notes. Add your own ideas.

1. When and where dances started

2. Kinds of dance

3. Kinds of movies

4. Phones and tablets for entertainment

2 Choose a project.

Organize an entertainment show.

1. Work in a small group. Put on an entertainment show for your class.
2. Decide what your group would like to perform, e.g. a play, a comedy, etc.
3. In your group, plan and decide what each person needs to say or do.
4. Practice. Then perform for the class.

or

Design a movie poster.

1. You're a movie director and you're going to make a movie.
2. Choose the title, music, characters, and storyline.
3. Design the poster for your movie.
4. Present the poster to the class.
5. Invite people to audition.

Read and circle for yourself.

I can understand details in dialogs.
I can understand someone's reasons.

I can make suggestions about what to do. I can talk about plans for the near furture.

I can identify key words and phrases. I can identify the writer's overall purpose.

I can give my opinion on a familiar topic.

9 Why are adventure stories popular?

Listening
- I can idenitfy opinions.
- I can understand key information.

Reading
- I can make predictions from headings.
- I can infer information.

Speaking
- I can talk about past events or experiences.

Writing
- I can write a simple story.

1 Look at the picture and discuss.

1 Who and what can you see in the picture?
2 How do you think the people on the ship feel?
3 Would you like to travel on this ship? Why?/Why not?

2 Look at the video still in Activity 3 and answer the questions. Then compare your answers with a friend.

1 What kind of ship is this? How do you know?
2 How would you describe the people who sailed on this ship?

3 ▶ 9-1 BBC Watch the video and answer.

1 Who was the most famous pirate in history?
2 Where did he sail? And with who?
3 When did he live?
4 What was his real name?
5 What did he do with the two different flags on the ship?

133

Pre-reading 1

1 💬 Discuss with a friend.

1 Do you know any famous sailors?
2 What do you know about them?
3 What would you like to find out about famous sailors?

> 📖 **Reading strategy**
>
> Use text headings to locate information efficiently.

2 💡 Read and answer. What information do you think you'll find under each heading? Which is the best heading for the text?

1 Nineteenth-century hero
2 Escaping the storm!
3 "It's what I do – I do the sea."
4 The best Christmas gift!
5 Space or sea?

> On April 24, 1895, Joshua Slocum sailed away from Boston Harbor in his boat, *The Spray*. Three years later he returned, after sailing 74,060 kilometers and becoming the first man to sail solo around the world. He visited many exciting places on his voyage, which he later wrote about in his famous book, *Sailing Alone Around the World*.

3 🎧 (2-22) Read *Sailing Around the World – Solo!*. Find out if your predictions for headings 2–5 are correct.

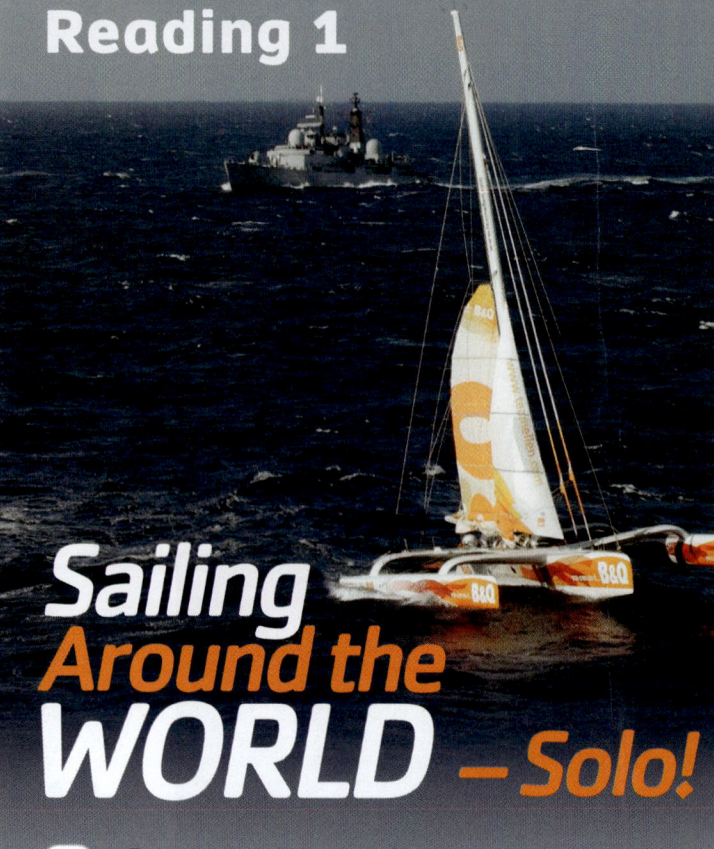

Reading 1

Sailing Around the WORLD – Solo!

1 Space or sea?

Did you know that more people have traveled to space than have sailed around the world alone? Sailing alone in a small boat or ship isn't easy – in fact, it's a huge **challenge**. Can you imagine what it would be like?

Read on to find out more about some of the brave sailors who have made this amazing journey.

2 "It's what I do – I do the sea."

These were the words of the English **yachtsman** Robin Knox-Johnston after his epic **solo** journey around the globe. In 1969, he became the first man to sail single-handed and **nonstop** around the world. His journey took 312 long days. The most difficult challenge for him was the **loneliness** – in those days there were no satellite phones, and after his radio broke he couldn't communicate with anyone for most of the journey. But he said, "To people it may seem dangerous, foolish even. But for me, it's where I'm happiest." And the most amazing thing is that he did it all again almost 40 years later when he was 68 years old!

3 The best Christmas gift!

The fastest man to **navigate** nonstop around the globe is a French yachtsman called Thomas Colville. He sailed 28,400 miles around the world in just 49 days. That's about seven weeks! His wife and son were waiting for him when he returned on December 25, 2016 – they said it was the best Christmas gift ever to have him home again. Sailing so quickly around the world was a real test of **endurance**. The biggest challenge was **exhaustion** – Thomas never slept for more than three hours at one time because he had to make sure the boat didn't **sink**. He also had to sail through monster waves up to 10 meters tall in the Indian Ocean. But there were great moments while he was sailing, too – when he saw dolphins, whales, and beautiful sunsets.

4 Escaping the storm!

Ellen MacArthur loved sailing from an early age. In 2004, she became the fastest woman to sail **solo** around the world, circumnavigating the globe in 71 days. On her journey she had to **battle** against **treacherous** icy oceans and terrifying winds. The worst moment was when she was sailing through the Southern Ocean close to Antarctica, with a huge storm behind her. At that moment she realized that she was completely alone, 2,000 miles from land. The closest people to her were in the European Space Station miles above her in space. It was a terrifying moment. Luckily, she escaped the storm and later, as she was looking at the beautiful calm, **moonlit** ocean, she realized just how lucky she was.

4 What do you think about the stories of yachtsmen and women sailing solo around the globe? Would you like to do it? Why?/Why not?

Comprehension 1

1 Read *Sailing Around the World – Solo!* again and answer.

1. Why do you think people sail around the world alone?
2. What are the best and worst things about sailing alone?

2 Read the sentences. Which paragraph from the text do they refer to? Write the number.

1. Ellen MacArthur battled against bad weather. ☐
2. Thomas Colville arrived home on December 25. ☐
3. Sailing alone is a huge challenge. ☐
4. Robin Knox Johnston is happiest in the ocean. ☐

3 Read and write the heading from the reading text where you can find the information below.

1. ....
   He didn't sleep very much.
   He saw dolphins and whales.

2. ....
   She's the fastest woman to sail solo around the world. She always loved sailing.

3. ....
   Not many people have sailed around the world alone.
   More people have traveled to space.

4. ....
   His journey took 312 days.
   He couldn't communicate with anyone.

Listening 1

4 Have you seen any movies or read any books about adventures in the ocean? Who were your favorite characters? Discuss with a friend.

> 🎧 **Listening strategy**
>
> Listen for opinions.

5 🎧 2-23 Listen to the conversation and circle.

1. The children are talking about **a book** / **a play** / **a movie**.
2. They enjoyed it **a bit** / **not much** / **a lot**.

6 🎧 2-24 Listen again and write *A* (Anja) or *F* (Filip).

1. My favorite character was Captain Coogan. ....
2. My favorite character was Sailor Maria. ....
3. My favorite scene was when they were watching the dolphins. ....
4. I loved it when they were sailing through the storm. ....
5. I like the ending, when they arrived home and met their families again. ....

7 Would you like to see *Adventures in the Ocean*? Why?/Why not?

Vocabulary 1

1 Find these words in *Sailing Around the World – Solo!* Circle the words that describe the difficulties of sailing alone around the world.

| battle | challenge | endurance | exhaustion | loneliness | navigate |
| nonstop | sink | solo | treacherous | moonlit | yachtsman |

2 🎧 2-25 Listen and say. Use the words from Activity 1.

3 Read and circle.

Laura Dekker was born on a boat and grew up on the ocean, so she was always a great ¹ **yachtswoman** / **explorer**. When she was only 16, she sailed alone – yes, ² **hard** / **solo** – around the world! She spent many weeks on her own, so she suffered from ³ **shyness** / **loneliness** during her trip. She was often very tired, so she had to deal with ⁴ **exhaustion** / **distance**, too. She had to ⁵ **ride** / **navigate** her boat through difficult and ⁶ **fine** / **treacherous** conditions. And she had to ⁷ **play** / **battle** against giant waves and storms. It was a real test of ⁸ **math** / **endurance**. But after a year and one day she made it! Now that's what I call a ⁹ **challenge** / **change**.

4 💬 Read and match. Compare with a friend. Can you make a sentence using each word in the first column?

1. a challenge
2. solo
3. to sink
4. to navigate
5. treacherous
6. exhaustion
7. endurance
8. to battle

a. feeling very tired
b. to fight or work very hard
c. having the strength to keep going
d. dangerous
e. alone
f. a difficulty
g. to go under water
h. to direct a boat on its way

5 💬 Read the questions. Discuss with a friend.

1. Why do you think there are so many books and movies about the ocean?
2. What makes stories about the ocean exciting?

Grammar 1

1 🎬 BBC 9-2 Watch Part 1 of the story video. Who does the Doctor speak to on the ship?

*The pirates weren't talking. They were fighting.
Doctor Who was watching them.*

2 🎬 BBC 9-3 Watch Part 2 of the story video. Then write **T** (true) or **F** (false).

1. Yellowbeard was trying to find his treasure. ....
2. Yellowbeard was a good pirate. ....
3. Mary Read was a bad pirate. ....
4. Doctor Who was helping Mary Read rescue her husband. ....

3 Read the grammar box and circle. Then write.

Grammar

I/He/She **was**/**wasn't sailing** to the island.
You/We/They **were**/**weren't sailing** to the island.

1. Yellowbeard's ship **was** / **were** sailing.
2. Mary Read's ship **were** / **was** following him.
3. Yellowbeard's eyes **wasn't** / **weren't** glowing red. They **was** / **were** glowing green.
4. The Smogsucker **wasn't** / **weren't** working. The Smogator **were** / **was** escaping.

Write the Progressive forms. Remember! What are the spelling rules?

swim – swim..........
have – hav..........

4 Read *Sailing Around the World – Solo!* again and circle examples of the *Past Progressive*. Think and check (✓). When do we use the *Past Progressive*?

for a short action in the past ☐
for a longer action in the past ☐

5 Look and write. What were they doing at six o'clock that evening?

	dance	eat	drink	sleeping
Pirates	✓	✗	✓	✗
Captain	✗	✓	✓	✗

At six o'clock that evening

1 the pirates *were dancing* .
2 they _____ .
3 they _____ .
4 they _____ .
5 the Captain _____ .
6 he _____ .
7 he _____ .
8 he _____ .

Speaking 1

6 What were you doing yesterday at six o'clock? Work in small groups and find someone who did the same.

At six o'clock yesterday I was helping my mom cook dinner. How about you?

I wasn't cooking dinner. I was doing my homework.

Pre-reading 2

1 💬 Discuss with a friend.

1. What kind of books do you like to read?
2. Do you like mysteries or adventure stories? Why?/Why not?

> 📖 **Reading strategy**
>
> Describe characters in a story.

2 💡 Read, think, and answer. Why do you think there's a strange light around the ship? Why do you think the Captain is waving at Tommy? What do you think will happen in the story?

> *Tommy was standing on the beach, looking out to the ocean. It was a stormy day – the sky was dark and the waves were crashing on the beach. Suddenly, Tommy saw a strange white light out in the ocean. Then he realised it was a ship, which was rocking up and down on the waves. The Captain was standing on the deck. His face was very white and he was waving at Tommy.*

3 🎧 2-26 Read *Pete and the Pirates*. Who does Pete meet?

Reading 2

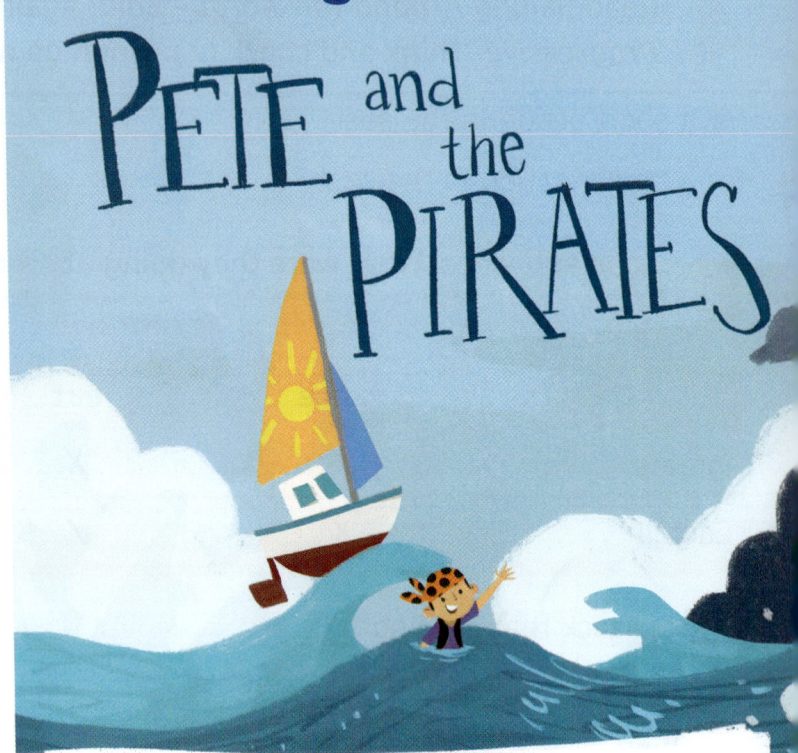

PETE and the PIRATES

Last summer, a young boy named Pete Morgan was visiting the Caribbean with his parents. They were staying on their boat, *Summer Sun*. Pete wasn't going to school, so his mum was teaching him. One morning she showed him a website called *Your family **history**!*

"History's boring!" said Pete. "Can I take my **metal detector** to the beach?"

"OK," said Mum. "You go to the beach, and I'll read up on our family history ready for our class later."

Pete took his metal detector to the beach to find some hidden treasure. But while he was searching for treasure, somebody was hiding behind a tree, watching him … It was a pirate!

Pete turned around to go home. A few minutes later, he saw the pirate, who was **pointing** a long **sword** at him.

"Who … who are you?" Pete asked **nervously**.

"I'm Tom," said the pirate. "Don't worry. Come with me, and bring your machine."

Pete was a little worried, but he followed Tom. The pirate led him to a big, white ship that was anchored close to the beach.

"That's my ship, the *White Rose*," said Tom.

"Are you a pirate?" asked Pete.

"Yes," said Tom. "I work on the *White Rose*."

"How exciting!" thought Pete.

Tom took Pete on board the *White Rose* to meet the Captain. He was old, with a long, grey beard and moustache. He had a black **eye patch** over one eye and a **scar** on his face.

"Our treasure is buried on an **island** near here, but we can't find it," said the Captain. "We only have one day. Can you and your machine help us?"

"Um … Yes," answered Pete.

So, what was Pete doing one hour later? He was searching for pirate treasure on the island with his metal detector. And what were the pirates doing? They were watching and waiting, excitedly. Suddenly they all heard … "Beeeep!" It was the treasure!

"Thank you, boy!" said the pirates. "Now you're a pirate too!"

But as they were taking the treasure back to the ship, there was a terrible storm. Pete looked at the dark sea and saw his boat, *Summer Sun*. It was bobbing up and down on the huge waves.

"Oh no! My boat!" he cried.

"Don't worry. Pirates help pirates," said the Captain.

He threw a long **rope** to Tom, who jumped into the water and swam out into the **huge** waves. Pete closed his eyes; he couldn't watch. But luckily Tom reached the boat and threw the rope back to the Captain. Together, they pulled *Summer Sun* back to the beach.

"Thank you!" said Pete. "What's your name, Captain?"

"Pete Morgan," said the Captain.

"That's my name too!" said Pete, surprised.

"I know! Come with me!" Pete showed Captain Morgan the history website on his computer.

"Look! You're my great-great-great-great-great-great-grandfather!" said Pete, smiling happily. The Captain smiled too, but it was getting dark, and the pirates had to return to the ship. Pete waved sadly as the *White Rose* sailed into the distance. Pete awoke with a start. "What a **mystery**, dreaming about pirates again," he said to himself.

Later in the day, Pete said, "Mum, can we study history tomorrow?"

"But I thought you didn't like history. You said it was boring!" said Mum.

"No, it isn't boring! It's fantastic!" said Pete.

4 Do you know any other famous pirate or adventure stories? Discuss with a friend.

Comprehension 2

1 Read *Pete and the Pirates* again and answer.

1. Are the pirates in the story real?
2. How does Pete help the pirates?
3. How do the pirates help Pete?
4. What does Pete find out about the Captain?

2 Read and number the sentences in order.

Pete helped the pirates find their treasure. ......

Pete saw that a pirate was watching him. ......

Pete met the Captain of the *White Rose*. ......

There was a storm, and the pirates rescued Pete's boat. ......

Pete found out that the Captain was a member of his family. ......

Pete was looking for treasure on the beach with his metal detector. ......

3 Find three words in the story to describe Pete and the Captain.

4 Answer the questions with a friend.

1. How do you think Pete felt when he first saw the *White Rose* and when he first met the Captain?
2. Why did the pirates tell Pete "Now you're a pirate, too!"?
3. Why does Pete like history at the end of the story?

Listening 2

> **Listening strategy**
>
> Listen for key information.

5 (2-27) Listen to the story. What was the *Mary Celeste*? Why is the story still a mystery?

6 (2-28) Listen again and circle.

1. Where did the *Mary Celeste* sail from?
   Italy / **New York** / **England**
2. How many people were on the ship when she set sail? **Ten** / **Seven** / **Five**
3. When the *Mary Celeste* was found, she was **sailing** / **sinking** / **drifting**.
4. There was enough food and water on the ship for **two** / **five** / **six** months.
5. How many people were on the ship when she was found? **None** / **Two** / **Ten**

7 What do you think happened to the *Mary Celeste*? Do you know any other strange stories about people or ships disappearing? Discuss with a friend.

Vocabulary 2

1 Find these words in *Pete and the Pirates*. What do you think they mean? Circle the verb.

> pointing   eye patch   huge   history
> island   metal detector   mystery   rope
> scar   sword   nervously

2 🎧 2-29 Listen and answer the questions. Use the words from Activity 1.

3 Read and complete the text. Use the words from Activity 1.

I love finding out about the past. I really like looking for old coins in the yard by ¹ .... my ² .... detector. And my favorite subject at school is ³ ....

I also like talking to my grandpa because he tells me stories about the past. He's old and he has a long, gray beard and a mustache. He has a bad eye, too, so he sometimes wears an ⁴ .... It makes him look like a pirate! He lives in a ⁵ .... house. When I stay there, I sometimes hear strange noises in the night. Last weekend, when I was staying with my grandpa, we went out on his boat. I ⁶ .... ! boarded the boat. We sailed out to an ⁷ .... Suddenly, water started coming into the boat! We thought the boat was going to sink. Luckily, a man on another boat threw us a ⁸ .... and rescued us. It was scary but fun!

4 Write words associated with each heading. Use the words from Activity 1.

Treasure
....
....
....

Pirate
....
....
....

Ship
....
....

5 💬 Discuss with a friend.

1 Do you like history? Why?/Why not?
2 Would you like to use a metal detector? What would you like to find?
3 Have you sailed on a ship or boat?

> I love history because I like learning about the past.

> I don't like history. I prefer to talk about what's happening today.

143

Grammar 2

1 Watch Part 3 of the story video. What was Mary Read doing? Then read and complete.

Where is the _____?

I know! I can _____ it with my Sonic Screwdriver!

2 Read the grammar box and circle.

3 Read *Pete and the Pirates* again. Circle questions in the *Past Progressive*. How do we make the question form of the *Past Progressive*?

Grammar

Was I/he/she/it **digging**?
Were you/we/they **digging**?

Yes, he/she/it **was**.
No, he/she/it **wasn't**.
Yes, you/we/they **were**.
No, you/we/they **weren't**.

1 **Was** / **Were** Yellowbeard's parents **live** / **living** on the island when he buried his treasure there?
2 Yes, they **were** / **weren't**.

4 Read and match. Then discuss with a friend.

1 Was Mary Read wearing boots?
2 Was she wearing an eye patch?
3 Were the pirates fighting?
4 Was Doctor Who holding a sword?
5 Were the pirates helping to find the treasure?

a No, he wasn't.
b Yes, she was.
c Yes, they were.
d No, they weren't.
e No, she wasn't.

144

5 Write the questions and then answer.

1 Captain's wife / sail / the boat
   .... ? Yes, she ....

2 the pirates / dig for treasure
   .... ? Yes, they ....

3 the ship / sink
   .... ? Yes, it ....

4 you / hide from me
   .... ? No, I ....

Speaking 2

6 Think about and write what you were doing at these times in the past. Discuss with a friend.

> **Speaking strategy**
> Try to find something in common with your friend.

Today 7:00 a.m.	
Today 8:30 a.m.	
Yesterday 12:00 p.m.	
Yesterday 4:00 p.m.	
Last Saturday 2:00 p.m.	
Last Sunday 6:00 p.m.	

What were you doing at seven o'clock this morning?

I was taking a shower. How about you?

I was taking a shower, too.

145

Writing

1 Scan the text. Answer the questions.

1. Is this a good beginning for a story? How else could you begin the story?
2. Can you describe the main character?
3. Would you like to continue reading the story? What do you think will happen next?

Santiago's ADVENTURE

Santiago was on holiday with his family. They went to the same place by the ocean every year, so he knew all the different coves and good places to hide. Santiago loved the beach and swimming in the ocean. He loved adventures and exploring!

It was a sunny day and Santiago woke early. The sun was streaming in through the window and he could see the surfers were already out searching for the perfect wave!

He dressed quickly and ate breakfast on the veranda with his mom. His mom had already packed him his favorite cheese sandwich and potato chips. His backpack was packed with all the essential things he needed for a day of adventure.

He raced out of the house, and down to the shore. His plan was to walk along the shore and walk to the next cove. Santiago was ready for an adventure!

2 Read the text. Check your answers from Activity 1.

3 Read the text again and think about:

- where the story takes place.
- who the main character is.
- what the main character is doing.

Writing strategy

Establish a context to your story and introduce characters.

4 WB 127 Find or draw pictures of your adventure story. Then go to the Workbook to do the writing activity.

Now I Know

1 Why are adventure stories popular? Look back through Unit 9. Use the information to answer the questions. Add your own ideas.

1 Why do you think people are interested in adventure stories?

....

2 What makes a good adventure story?

....

2 Choose a project.

Research a famous sailor.

1 Work with a friend and choose a famous explorer.
2 Find out as much as you can about them, using reference books or the internet.
3 Find pictures of your explorer.
4 Make a presentation showing what you have found out. Present to the class.

or

Write a review of a book or a movie about adventure.

1 Choose a book or movie.
2 Who are the main characters? What's the story about?
3 Did you like the movie? Why?/Why not? Would you recommend it?
4 Write your review. Present to the class.

Read and circle for yourself.

I can identify opinions. I can understand key information.

I can make predictions from headings. I can infer information.

I can talk about past events or experiences.

I can write a simple story.

10 Why do we raise money for charity?

Listening
- I can understand details in dialogs.
- I can understand key information in recorded materials.

Reading
- I can identify key vocabulary and expressions.
- I can understand the main ideas in stories.

Speaking
- I can talk about personal experiences and past events.

Writing
- I can write notices about events.

1 💬 **Look at the picture and discuss.**

1 Who can you see in the picture?
2 What are they doing?
3 Why do you think they're doing it?

2 **Look at the video still in Activity 3 and answer the questions. Then compare your answers with a friend.**

1 What can you see?
2 What do you think the people are doing?

3 ▶ 10-1 BBC **Watch the video and check your answers from Activity 2. Then watch again and answer the questions.**

1 What does Bristol FareShare do?
2 Who benefits from the food?
3 Why is the food donated? Is there anything wrong with it?
4 How many volunteers work at Bristol FareShare?
5 What does Maddie mean by working together as a community?

Pre-reading 1

1 💬 Discuss with a friend.

1. What charities do you know about?
2. Does your school do anything to help a charity? If so, what?

> 📖 **Reading strategy**
>
> Determine the meaning of specific words and phrases in a text.

2 💡 Read and answer. What charity does the school want to support?

> This year at our school we're going to support a charity that helps endangered animals, such as the Asian elephant and the marine turtle. It's called the *World Wide Fund for Nature*. WWF has projects all around the world and they need our help to carry on with their important work.
>
> We'd like to hear your ideas about how we can raise money for this amazing charity.

3 🎧 3-01 Read *What Is Biblioburro?* What charity is the school going to support?

150

Reading 1

Archdale Primary School

Our charity page

This year at Archdale Primary School, we're raising money for a **charity** called Biblioburro. Look at the **website** to find out more about this charity and to see what our school is doing to **support** it.

What Is Biblioburro?

Biblioburro is a travelling library that takes books to children who can't easily go to school. It was started in the late 1990s by Luis Soriano, a primary school teacher from Colombia. Luis understood how difficult it was for some children living in remote and poor areas of Colombia to go to school – some children had to walk or ride a donkey for up to 40 minutes to get to school.

He knew that he had to take books out to these children to help them learn. So, he asked people to donate books. He loaded the books up on his two donkeys, Alfa and Beto. Then he rode out to schools and small towns in remote regions, delivering the books to children who couldn't go to school. He started with a small collection of about 70 books. He now has thousands of books, but he needs more!

The charity is now building a small library to keep all the books that people donate. That's why it needs our help.

How can we help?

Donate!

We are asking each family to **donate** a book. If you have a book that you've read, but no longer need, please bring it in! We have collection buckets in each classroom, so please put your books in the bucket!

Volunteer!

Have you or your parents got extra time on your hands? You could come to the library and help us pack the donated books before we send them out to Biblioburro. If you can help **regularly**, for example once a week, that would be great! If not, then you can just come and help whenever you've got some free time.

If you or your parents would like to **volunteer**, please tell your class teacher. Or you can phone us, send a **text message** 💬 or **email** ✉.

Raise money!

We are organising a sponsored walk to **raise money** for Biblioburro. We want as many children as possible to take part. We're going to walk from the school to the park and back again. Get your family and friends to **sponsor** you! Come and join us on the walk, then collect the money from your friends and family.

We're also asking each class to organise a special event. Can you bake? Maybe you could bake some cakes and do a cake sale? Or perhaps you can sing or play a musical instrument? You could organise a mini concert in your class and ask for donations.

And finally, this Friday is "Mad Hair Day!" Come to school wearing your own clothes and a mad hairstyle. We'd like everyone to donate £1 on the day.

We think Biblioburro is a really important charity because it aims to help children develop a love of reading. Help us raise money if you can!

4 💡 Is this a charity you would like to support? Why?/Why not?

Comprehension 1

1 Read *What Is Biblioburro?* again and answer.

1 What is Biblioburro? Who was it founded by and when was it founded?
2 Why does the school want to support this charity?

2 Read and circle.

1 Some children in Colombia don't go to school because they **don't want to / live too far away from the closest school**.
2 Biblioburro is helping by **training teachers / taking books out to children**.
3 Luis Soriano delivers the books **on a donkey / in a truck**.
4 The charity is now building a **new stable for the donkeys / library to keep books in**.

3 Check (✓) the ways Archdale Primary School wants to support Biblioburro.

asking children to donate books ☐
drawing pictures ☐
raising money ☐
sending toys ☐
building a school ☐
doing a sponsored walk ☐
asking people to volunteer ☐

Listening 1

4 Do you and your family support any charities?

> **Listening strategy**
> Listen for information.

5 (3-02) Listen to the interview. Which charities do the Garcia family support?

**Misión México   Red Cross
a food bank**

6 (3-03) Listen again and circle.

1 Julio's favorite charity knows how to help **children / animals**.
2 Julio did a sponsored **walk / run** to raise money for his favorite charity.
3 Señora Garcia volunteers in a **food bank / grocery store**.
4 Señor Garcia knows how to design **websites / toys**.
5 Señor Garcia answers **letters / emails** from people.

7 Would you support either of these charities? Why?/Why not?

152

Vocabulary 1

1 Find these words in *What Is Biblioburro?*. Which words describe what children and their parents can do to help the charity?

> charity   donate   email
> raise money   regularly   sponsor
> support   text message
> volunteer   website

2 🎧 3-04 Listen and say. Use the words from Activity 1.

3 Read and match.

1. My mom volunteers in a food bank.
2. I donate to a charity.
3. I look at the internet regularly.
4. The charity has a page on the internet.
5. My friends sponsored me for charity.
6. My dad raises money for charity.

a. I look at it every day.
b. They gave me money for doing an activity for charity.
c. I give $5 a month.
d. He helps to get money for charity.
e. She gives her time for free.
f. The charity has a website.

4 Read and complete the text. Use the words from Activity 1.

🐾 ANIMAL Aid

Animal Aid is a ¹ .... that helps animals in need. There are a lot of things you can do to help us ² .... money. You could ³ .... $10 every month. Or if you have some free time, you could ⁴ .... in one of our stores. If you know how to design internet pages, you could help us with our ⁵ .... Or if you're good at sports, you could ask your friends to ⁶ .... you to do a run or walk for charity. Please help us if you can. We need your ⁷ ....

5 💬 Discuss with a friend.

1. What websites do you look at regularly?
2. Do you write emails or text messages? Who to? When?
3. Does anyone in your family volunteer for a charity?

Grammar 1

1 Watch Part 1 of the story video. Who's Sally trying to help? Then read and complete.

Ah! I have an idea. I .... how to find some more help on the internet.

2 Watch Part 1 of the story video again and answer.

1 How can Sally help them?
2 What does she do?

3 Read the grammar box and match.

Grammar

I/You/We **know/understand how to** help.
I/You/We **don't know/understand how to** help.
He/She **knows/understands how to** help.
He/She **doesn't know/understand how to** help.
Do you **know/understand how to** help?
Does he/she **know/understand how to** help?

1 Sally's grandparents   a how to send a text message.
2 Sally knows   b understands how to use the internet to get help.
3 Sally   c don't know how to get help.

4 Read *What Is Biblioburro?* and circle examples of *know* and *understand how to*.

154

5 Read and complete the text. Use *know/understand how to*.

My grandparents are pretty old and they don't ¹ .... use technology. My grandma ² .... bake a cake, but she ³ .... use the internet. My grandpa can fix a car, but he doesn't ⁴ .... fix the computer. But there are some things my grandparents ⁵ .... do that I don't. I ⁶ .... knit a sweater like my grandma, and I ⁷ .... play cards like my grandpa.

6 Write questions. Then write answers for you.

1 you / know / send a text message
   ....? ....

2 you / know / design a website
   ....? ....

3 your grandpa / understand / write an email
   ....? ....

4 your parents / understand / help you with your homework
   ....? ....

Speaking 1

7 What do you know how to do? Use the ideas below and your own ideas. Discuss with a friend.

Speaking strategy

Think when it's your turn to speak.

design a website
search for something on the internet
send a text message
write an email

Do you know how to write an email?

Yes, I do. Do you understand how to design a website?

155

Pre-reading 2

1 💬 Discuss with a friend. What chores do you do at home to help your family?

> 📖 **Reading strategy**
>
> Compare your life to that of characters to understand a story about a different culture.

2 💡 Read, think, and answer. What does Sahil have to do to help his family? Why does he have to do it? Would you like to live like Sahil? Why?/Why not?

Sahil woke up very early every day. He had to make breakfast for the family, sweep the house, then head out to the garbage dump before eight o'clock. He spent all day at the garbage dump, looking for things he and his family could use or sell. Sahil was only nine years old, but his family was poor, and he had to help bring in some money.

3 🎧 3-05 Read *Miremba's Dream Comes True*. Find out what Miremba has to do to help her family.

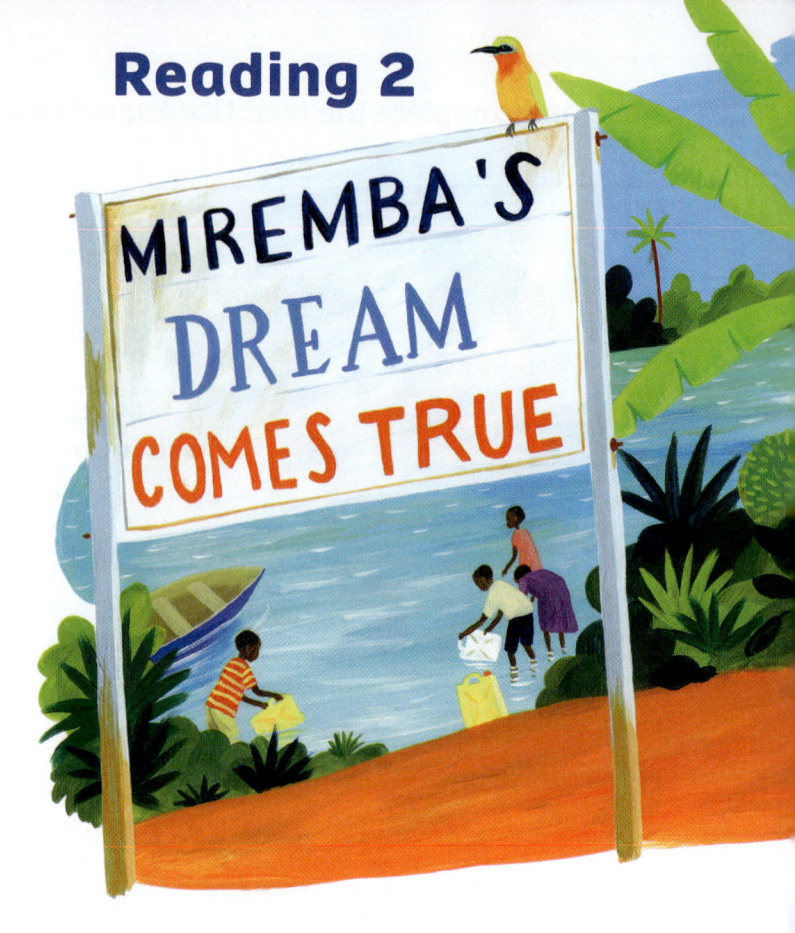

Reading 2

MIREMBA'S DREAM COMES TRUE

It was early morning in the settlement. Miremba was getting out of bed when she heard her mother call.

"Miremba, you must go to the river today. We need water for cooking and washing."

"Alright, Mother," sighed Miremba. She was tired and didn't want to walk to the river. She wanted to go to school to **improve** her reading and writing instead. But the family needed water, and Miremba's mother couldn't go to the river – she had to take care of the younger children, and to **care for** Miremba's sick grandparents. So Miremba had to go and collect the water.

"I wish we had a faucet in the house. Or even just a water **well** in the settlement," she thought, as she picked up the **jerry can** and headed out of the door.

The journey to the river and back took many hours and was sometimes dangerous. Coming face to face with wild animals was a **constant** worry. So Miremba **frequently** walked to the river with her friend, Akiki.

10

There were some visitors in the settlement. They said they were from an **organization** called *Schools for Wells*. They gathered everyone together and read a letter aloud. It was from some schoolchildren in England. "Hello, everyone. Our teacher, Ms. Diaz, visited your settlement last year. She told us all about her trip and she said that you needed a well in your settlement. So, we decided to raise some money to help you. We got together with some other schools, and we did a big sponsored run. We had a collection, too, and everyone contributed. We're happy to say that we **collected** enough money to help you build a well in your settlement. We hope you enjoy your well and that you will now be able to go to school and learn to read and write!"

That day, while they were walking to the river, Miremba heard a hissing noise in the long grass. "Stop! Be quiet!" whispered Miremba. The girls stood very still, their hearts beating like drums as they watched a long snake slither by their feet, just inches away. "Phew!" they sighed. "That was close."

While they were walking to the river, the girls also talked about their dreams for the future. "I want to be a doctor one day," said Akiki. "I want to be a teacher," dreamed Miremba. "But we have to spend so much time collecting water, there's no time to study. I wish we had a well in the settlement!" she sighed.
"Me, too," said Akiki.
"Do you remember that lady from England who visited last year?" asked Miremba.
"Yes, she was very **helpful** and said she would try to get us a well," answered Akiki. "Do you think she's forgotten us?"
"Maybe," sighed Miremba.

However, later that day when Miremba and Akiki returned home, they had a big surprise.

"Ms. Diaz! She did remember us!" exclaimed Miremba. "I can't believe that those schoolchildren have been so **generous**!"
"We're going to have a well! We'll be able to go to school every day!" shouted Akiki happily.
"Maybe we'll be teachers and doctors one day!"
"Yes, and one day soon we'll be able to write a letter to Ms. Diaz and her schoolchildren to say thank you for our well!" said Miremba.

4 Do you think Miremba's dream of becoming a teacher came true? Why?/Why not?

Comprehension 2

1 Read *Miremba's Dream Comes True* again and write **T** (true) or **F** (false).

1 Miremba had a faucet in her house. ....
2 Miremba went to school every day. ....
3 Miremba had to help with chores. ....
4 Miremba enjoyed collecting water every day. ....

2 Compare your life to Miremba's. Read and circle.

1 **I go** / **Miremba goes** to school every day.
2 **I have** / **Miremba has** running water at home.
3 **I can't** / **Miremba can't** go to school.
4 **I walk** / **Miremba walks** to the river every day.
5 **I dream** / **Miremba dreams** about being a teacher.

Listening 2

> 🎧 **Listening strategy**
> Listen for who's speaking.

3 🎧 3-06 Listen to the talk. Who's speaking? Who's he speaking to?

4 🎧 3-07 Listen again and match.

1 Jonas works for an international
2 He's talking to some children at their
3 The charity helps old people who don't have families to
4 Most children at the school have
5 He suggests that they can do a sponsored run or

a grandparents.
b a cupcake sale.
c organization.
d school.
e care for them.

5 💬 Do you agree that grandparents are an important part of our families? Why?/Why not? How do you help your grandparents? Discuss with a friend.

Vocabulary 2

1 Find these words in *Miremba's Dream Comes True*. What do you think they mean?

> care for   collect   constant
> frequently   generous   helpful   improve
> jerry can   organization   well

2 🎧 3-08 Listen and say. Use the words from Activity 1.

3 Read and circle.

My mom and dad both have very busy jobs. My mom works in a hospital. She **¹ cares for / collects** sick children. My dad works for a large **² organize / organization**. Mom and Dad **³ frequently / constant** have to work late, so everyone in our house has to contribute to doing chores around the house. I try to be **⁴ helping / helpful** by keeping my room clean and neat. And I sometimes **⁵ collect / give** my younger sister from school. Other times my grandparents come and take care of us if Mom and Dad are late at work. I like it when they come. They're very **⁶ poor / generous** and always bring us candy and toys!

4 Complete the chart. Use the words from the box.

> collect   improve   generous
> helpful   jerry can   organization

Thing or person (noun)	Doing word (verb)	Describing word (adjective)

5 💬 Read the questions. Discuss with a friend.

1. What or who do you help/care for, e.g. a pet/grandparents/younger brothers or sisters?
2. Do you think you're helpful at home? How could you be more helpful?
3. What activities do you do frequently?

Grammar 2

1 🎬 10-3 BBC Watch Parts 2 and 3 of the story video. What did the Doctor and Jack decide to do to raise money?

> Look! We have an email asking for help.

2 🎬 10-4 BBC Watch Parts 2 and 3 of the story video again and answer.

1. What does Jack remember from the past?
2. What does he put in his pocket? Why?
3. What makes the work easier?
4. How do they improve the home?

3 Read the grammar box and complete.

Grammar

I/He/She **was looking** on the internet when I/he/she **found** the picture.
You/We/They **were looking** on the internet when you/we/they **found** it.

1. While Jack _____ (think) about the past, he remembered the internet.
2. He was thinking how to raise money when he _____ (have) an idea.
3. Jack _____ (make) cakes when he found the last clue.

4 Read *Miremba's Dream Comes True* again. Circle examples of the *Past Progressive* and *Past Simple*. Then read and circle.

1. The Past Progressive describes a **long** / **short** activity in the past.
2. The Past Simple describes a **long** / **short** activity in the past.

160

5 Read and circle.

1 Yesterday, I **was surfing** / **surfed** the internet when it crashed.
2 The volunteers **started** / **were starting** the project two years ago.
3 My grandma **sent** / **was sending** me an email last week.
4 She **was daydreaming** / **daydreamed** when she **had** / **was having** an idea.
5 My mom **donated** / **was donating** $200 to her favorite charity last year.

6 Write four sentences using the *Past Progressive* and *Past Simple*. Use the ideas in the boxes.

do a sponsored run
play in the yard
visit the zoo
walk through the forest

find some treasure
hear a strange noise
meet a tiger
slip on a banana skin

1 While I .... , I ....
2 She .... when ....
3 They .... when ....
4 ....

Speaking 2

7 💬 Discuss with a friend. Use the *Past Progressive* and *Past Simple*. Use the ideas from Activity 6 or add some of your own to come up with a short story.

I was playing in the yard when …

… I met a tiger!

Writing

1 Scan the text. Answer the questions.

1. What's the event?
2. Why is the event taking place?
3. Would you like to take part in this event? Why?/Why not?

CAKE SALE

WHEN: 2:00 P.M., THURSDAY, APRIL 20TH

WHERE: THE SCHOOL CAFETERIA

WHO: EVERYONE IS WELCOMED!

Are you interested in helping a charity? Do you know how to make cupcakes? Do you know how to sell things?

If you know how to do these things, come and help at our Cake Sale event. Help us raise money for **Houses for the Homeless!**

If you don't know how to make cupcakes, don't worry. Just come along and donate some money for this important charity.

2 Read the text. Check your answers from Activity 1.

3 Read the text again and complete the chart.

When	Where	Who

Writing strategy

Write an informative text to convey information clearly. Think about **when**, **where**, and **who** to convey the information clearly.

*Come along to the sponsored run **on Friday at the park.***

4 (WB 141) Find or draw pictures for your event. Then go to the Workbook to do the writing activity.

Now I Know

1 Why do we raise money for charity? Look back through Unit 10. Use the information to answer the questions. Add your own ideas.

1 How do charities raise money?

....

2 How do they use technology to help them do this?

....

2 Choose a project.

Plan a fund-raising campaign for a charity.

1 Work in a group. Choose a charity you want to raise money for.
2 Decide on events you can organize, plan your events, and make a poster.
3 Present your ideas to the class.

or

Review a charity website. What makes a good website? Why?

1 Choose a charity and look at its website.
2 Think about the good and bad points of the website, e.g. the design, the amount of information, etc.
3 Write your review of the website.

Read and circle for yourself.

I can understand details in dialogs. I can understand key information in recorded materials.

I can identify key vocabulary and expressions. I can understand the main ideas in stories.

I can talk about personal experiences and past events.

I can write notices about events.

11

How are we similar but different?

Listening
- I can identify opinions.
- I can understand details in extended dialogs.

Reading
- I can identify supporting details.
- I can draw simple conclusions.

Speaking
- I can talk about personal experiences.
- I can describe similarities between appearances.

Writing
- I can describe similarities between two people.

1 💬 **Look at the picture and discuss.**

1 Who can you see in the picture?
2 Are the children happy?
3 Do you think the children are classmates?
4 Do you enjoy spending time with your classmates?
5 What do you do with your classmates?

2 **Look at the video still in Activity 3 and answer the questions. Then compare your answers with a friend.**

1 What can you see in the picture?
2 Do you think they're good friends? Why?/Why not?

3 ▶ 11-1 BBC **Watch the video and answer.**

1 What kinds of friends are there?
2 What does being a good friend mean to the interviewees?
3 What tips do they give for making friends?
4 What tips would you give someone for making new friends at your school?

165

Pre-reading 1

1 💬 Discuss with a friend.

1. Do you know any stories or books about friendship?
2. Who are the main characters?
3. How do they become friends?

> 📖 **Reading strategy**
>
> Look for adjectives to understand the characters better.

2 Read and choose two qualities that describe the girl in the story. Compare your answers in pairs.

friendly	kind	naughty
polite	poor	rich	shy

CHAPTER 1
Anne Arrives in Avonlea

Matthew Cuthbert drove to the station. There was only one person there, a little girl about eleven years old. She was thin, with large, gray eyes, and long, red hair. She wore a short, ugly dress and carried an old bag.

When she saw Matthew, she smiled and put out her hand. "Hello, I'm Anne!" she said. "I'm from the orphanage."

3 🎧 3-09 Read *Anne of Green Gables*. What else do you find out about Anne's character?

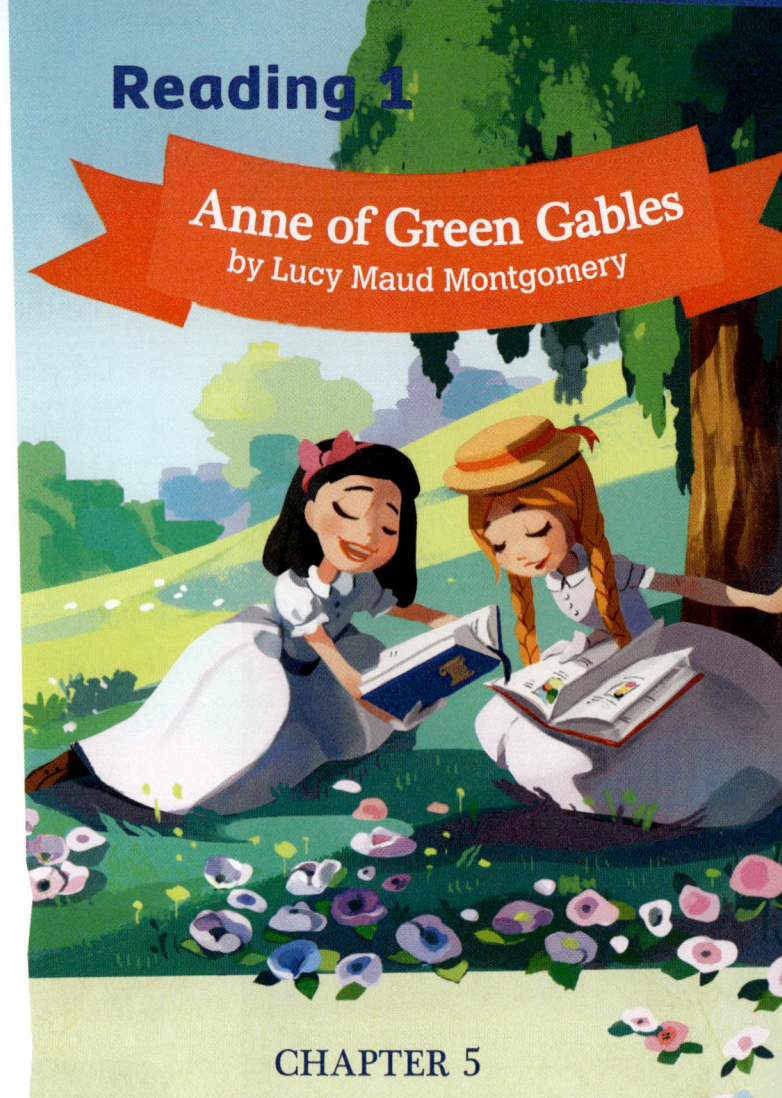

Reading 1

Anne of Green Gables
by Lucy Maud Montgomery

CHAPTER 5
Friends and Enemies

"Marilla," asked Anne, "do any other girls live close to Green Gables? I'd like to have a best friend."

"Yes," answered Marilla. "I **think** you'd like Diana Barry. She's a kind and **thoughtful** girl. Should we go and see her?"

Diana was a pretty girl with black hair and dark eyes. She looked very different from Anne, who had red hair and gray eyes. The girls went out into the yard. They were both shy at first, but Anne was a **talkative** girl and couldn't stay quiet for long. They soon found they **had something in common** – they both loved reading. They talked about books all afternoon. And Anne, being an **imaginative** girl with a great mind, told Diana a lot of stories.

That day, Anne and Diana agreed to be best friends. They promised to be **honest** and **open** and never to tell lies or keep secrets.

"We'll always be friends and nobody will ever come between us!" they **vowed**.

After that, Anne and Diana met every day. They played in the woods, read books, and told stories. They always had a wonderful time.

Then summer ended, and Anne and Diana had to go to school. Anne was good at her classes and she liked the other girls. But she didn't like the teacher, Mr. Phillips.

One day, a new boy arrived at school. "That's Gilbert Blythe," said Diana. Gilbert was tall, with black hair. The girls liked him because he was smart and funny. He could make everybody laugh.

Gilbert's desk was close to Anne's. He often looked at her, and he wanted her to look at him, too. But Anne wasn't interested in Gilbert.

One day, Gilbert took a handful of Anne's hair and held it up, shouting, "Carrots! Carrots!" Anne jumped up and looked at Gilbert angrily. "I hate you! I hate you!" she cried. She hit Gilbert over the head with her slate, and the slate broke. Everybody looked at her.

"Anne! What do you think you're doing?" shouted Mr. Phillips.

"Anne didn't do anything wrong," said Gilbert quickly. "I was acting **arrogantly** and rudely about her hair."

"Anne, go and stand in front of the class," said Mr. Phillips.

Anne stood in front of the class all afternoon. Everybody looked at her, but she didn't look at anybody. "Gilbert Blythe is **mean**," she thought. "I hate him!"

After school, Gilbert tried to talk to Anne, but she walked past him.

The next day after lunch, the children arrived late for school. Anne ran in laughing, with flowers in her hair. Mr. Phillips was angry and told her to sit next to Gilbert. Anne did as she was told, but she didn't look at Gilbert or talk to him. A little later, Gilbert tried to make friends again by giving Anne some candy. But Anne was **stubborn**. She threw the candy on the ground and wouldn't talk to Gilbert.

At the end of the day, Anne was **feeling** upset and angry. She picked up her slate and books, and marched out of the schoolroom.

"What are you doing?" asked Diana, surprised.

"I'm taking my things home. I'll learn my lessons there. I'm not coming back to school."

4 Think about your best friends. Where and how did you meet? What do you like doing together?

Comprehension 1

1 Read *Anne of Green Gables* again and answer.

1. Why do you think Anne and Diana became friends?
2. Why didn't Anne like Gilbert?

2 Read and write **T** (true) or **F** (false).

1. Anne and Diana became best friends slowly. ....
2. At school, nobody liked Gilbert. ....
3. Gilbert wanted to be friends with Anne. ....
4. Anne had strong feelings and gets angry quickly. ....

3 Write the words that describe each character.

> imaginative   funny   kind
> pretty   rude   smart
> stubborn   talkative

1. Anne: ....
2. Diana: ....
3. Gilbert: ....

4 Imagine you're Diana or Gilbert. Describe your first meeting with Anne. What happened from your character's point of view?

Listening 1

5 What do you think are the most important qualities in a friend?

Listening strategy
Listen for opinions.

6 (3-10) Listen to the conversation. What are the children talking about?

7 (3-11) Listen again. Check (✓) to show what each child thinks is important in a friend.

	Miguel	Antonio	Rosa
Being honest			
Liking the same things			
Having fun			
Being kind and polite			
Being different			
Being creative			

8 Who do you agree with most? Miguel, Antonio, or Rosa? Why? Discuss with a friend.

Vocabulary 1

1 Find these words in *Anne of Green Gables*. Which qualities do you think are important in a friend?

| arrogant | feeling | funny | have something in common | honest | imaginative |
| mean | open | rude | stubborn | talkative | think | thoughtful | vow |

2 🎧 3-12 Listen and say. Use the words from Activity 1.

3 Read and circle.

1 My mom says I never stop talking. I'm very **talkative** / **quiet** / **shy**.
2 My friend likes telling us stories. He's **helpful** / **imaginative** / **kind**.
3 My brother says horrible things to me. He's so **brave** / **polite** / **mean**.
4 My sister talks to everyone about her feelings. She's very **open** / **shy** / **naughty**.
5 I never tell lies. I always tell the truth. I'm very **mean** / **true** / **honest**.

4 Read and complete. Use *think* or *feel*.

1 What's the highest mountain in the world?
I'm not sure, but I .... it's Everest.

2 Hi, Gemma! How are you?
I'm .... nervous. I have an exam today.

3 Do you like my kitten?
Yes, I love it! Its fur .... so soft!

5 💬 Discuss with a friend.

1 What do you have in common with your friends?
2 What do you think about when you're alone?
3 How do you feel when you meet new people?

Grammar 1

1 Watch Part 1 of the story video. Answer the questions. Then read and complete.

I think I can see ....

1 What's Stonehenge?
2 How did they find the X?
3 How deep do they dig?
4 What do they find?

2 Look at the grammar box and read.

Grammar

He's so rich he can buy **anything** he wants.
Is there **anyone** in your family who has red hair?
Do you want to buy **something** from the supermarket?
I went to the park, but there wasn't **anybody** there.
Let's find **someone** who can help us.
I knew **nothing** about today's meeting.
She knocked on the door, but **no one** answered.
I felt that **everything** was going wrong.
Everyone had fun at the party last night.

People
somebody/someone
everybody/everyone
nobody/no one
anybody/anyone

Things
something
everything
nothing
anything

3 Read *Anne of Green Gables* again and circle examples of words beginning with *some-* ... , *any-* ... , or *every-* ... . What do these kinds of words describe?

a one particular person or thing
b no particular person or thing

4 Read and circle.

1 **Everyone** / **Everything** had fun at the party.
2 I didn't know **anybody** / **nobody** on my first day at my new school.
3 Listen! Did you hear **something** / **everything**?
4 Do you know **anything** / **anyone** about science?
5 There was **nobody** / **anybody** at home when I arrived.
6 I don't know **nothing** / **anything** about chess.
7 My music teacher taught me **everything** / **everyone** I know about music.
8 Look! I think there's **somebody** / **everybody** in the yard.

5 Read, choose, and write.

> anything   everything   everyone   nobody
> nothing   something   someone

Yesterday my English teacher asked me to prepare a presentation to the class about my favorite hobby. I'm shy, so I felt very nervous about it. Last night, ¹ _____ strange happened. I imagined I was standing in front of the class and ² _____ was looking at me. But I couldn't think of ³ _____ to say. Finally, I started talking, but ⁴ _____ listened to me. They all started shouting, and there was ⁵ _____ I could do to make them stop. Then I suddenly heard ⁶ _____ saying, "Sonia, wake up!" I opened my eyes and saw my mom standing next to my bed. I realized that it was just a bad dream and that ⁷ _____ was going to be alright.

Speaking 1

6 Imagine you're going on vacation. Think about what you would like to know. Then discuss with a friend.

Tell me **something** you know about London.

The Queen of England lives there.

Do you know **anything** else?

I'm afraid this is **everything** I know.

Pre-reading 2

1 💬 Discuss with a friend.

1 What do you look like?
2 Do you look like anyone in your family?

> 📖 **Reading strategy**
>
> Describe scientific ideas in a text to understand them better.

2 Read and answer. Who are Rodrigo and Santi? What do they look like? Do they have anything in common?

👥 Rodrigo and Santi 👥

I'm Rodrigo and this is my brother, Santi. People say we look like each other. We've got black hair and dark eyes. We've got small noses and round faces. We're quite like each other too. We're both quite shy and quiet. And we've got a lot in common – we both like listening to music and playing football – I suppose that's because we grew up together and did the same things as children.

3 🎧 3-13 Read *Nature or Nurture?*. Find out why people in a family often look similar.

Reading 2

Nature or Nurture?

Who do you look like? 👁

Think about what you look like. What colour eyes have you got? Have you got straight or curly hair? Are you tall or short?

Do people ever say, "You look just like your mum!" or "Your eyes are just like your dad's!"?

Everybody is **unique** – no two people are exactly the same. But we often look **similar** to one of our parents or to someone in our family.

People say I look like my mum – we have both got blue eyes and straight blonde hair. I'm quite like her in other ways too. My mum is very **active**. She's always doing things and does lots of sport and that's why I love sport too. And we're both **forgetful** – I'm always forgetting things and so is she.
Mia, 12

People tell me I look like my dad. We have both got dark hair and brown eyes. I think we're quite similar in other ways. My dad is very **practical** – he makes lots of things and he grows vegetables too. He teaches me to make things, so I think I'm learning to be practical like him.
Rodrigo, 11

The Science...

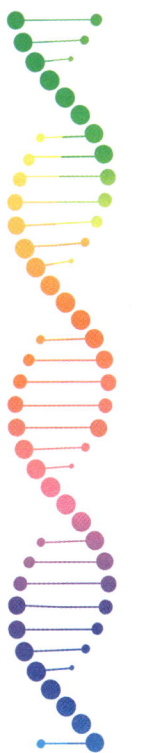

We've all got a special molecule in our bodies called DNA. And every molecule of DNA has got sections called genes. The genes are like a code – they give instructions to our cells, telling them how to grow and what job to do. Scientists agree that our DNA and our genes **determine** things like our eye colour or hair colour, and whether we are tall or short. We all get half of our DNA from our mum and half from our dad. That's why we often look like our parents.

But what about our **character** or personality? Does DNA determine that too?

The answer is that our DNA probably determines some of our character and some of our talents. So, if your dad is very musical, then you may be too. Or if your mum is very creative, then you may have got the same "creative" genes.

But there's another reason why we're like our parents – we learn how to **respond** to different situations by watching how our parents **behave**.

So, if your see that your parents are happy and positive, you learn to be happy and **positive** too.
Or if they get angry quickly, then you may learn to do the same.

Nature or Nurture?

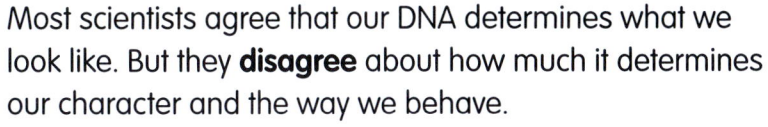

Most scientists agree that our DNA determines what we look like. But they **disagree** about how much it determines our character and the way we behave.

Some scientists think our DNA determines everything about us. Others think the environment we grow up in determines how we are. The truth is that it's probably a bit of both.

This is a DNA molecule.

Fun Facts

More than 99.9 percent of our DNA is the same as other people's. The other 0.1 percent is unique to you!

We share 98 percent of our DNA with chimpanzees and 50 percent with bananas!

4 Who do you look like in your family? Who are you most like in character?

173

Comprehension 2

1 Read *Nature or Nurture?* again and circle.

1 You would find this text in a **newspaper** / **science magazine** / **letter**.
2 The purpose of the text is to **make you laugh** / **give you information** / **tell you a story**.

2 Read and write **T** (true) or **F** (false).

1 No two people are exactly the same. ....
2 We often look similar to someone in our family. ....
3 Mia has blond hair like her dad. ....
4 Rodrigo and his dad both have brown eyes. ....
5 Mia and her mom are both lazy. ....
6 Rodrigo and his dad both enjoy making things. ....

3 Read and complete.

1 We all have a special molecule in our bodies called ....
2 Our genes determine things like .... color and .... color.
3 DNA probably determines some of our character and ....
4 We also learn to behave in certain ways by watching our ....
5 We share 98 percent of our DNA with ....

4 What do you understand by *Nature or Nurture?*. Discuss with a friend.

Listening 2

> **Listening strategy**
> Listen for similarities.

5 🎧 3-14 Listen to the conversation. Who's talking? What are they talking about?

6 🎧 3-15 Listen again and circle.

1 Mom found a picture of her **grandparents** / **parents**.
2 Mom and her grandma both have **curly** / **straight** hair.
3 Everyone in the family is pretty **stubborn** / **creative**.
4 Mom's grandpa was **tall** / **short** and handsome.
5 Sam thinks he's like his great-grandpa because he's **practical** / **funny**.
6 Sam and Lola's great-grandpa was **hardworking** / **positive**.

7 What do you know about past generations of your family? Are you like them? Do you look like them? Discuss with a friend.

Vocabulary 2

1 Find these words in *Nature or Nurture?*. Circle the adjectives (describing words). Underline the verbs (action words). Which word isn't an adjective or a verb?

> active   behave   character   determine
> disagree   forgetful   positive   practical
> respond   similar   unique

2 Look at the words from Activity 1. Which adjective describes someone who:

1 is always forgetting things? _____
2 is good at making things? _____
3 is always happy and cheerful? _____
4 is not the same as anyone else? _____

3 Read and match.

1 If you don't behave,   a but she didn't respond.
2 My mom and dad disagree   b she's kind and thoughtful.
3 She has a good character;   c whether you move to the next level.
4 Your scores will determine   d about where to go on vacation.
5 I asked my mom a question,   e you'll get into trouble.

4 💬 Discuss with a friend.

1 What places do you have to behave well in? How? Why?
2 Which of these words best describe your character: practical, active, creative, positive, forgetful? Why?
3 Do you often disagree with your friends or family? Why?/Why not?
4 Who in your family are you most like?
5 Describe your friend's character? What do you like about your friend?

175

Grammar 2

1 Watch Parts 2 and 3 of the story video. Who can you see in the photo album? Then answer the questions.

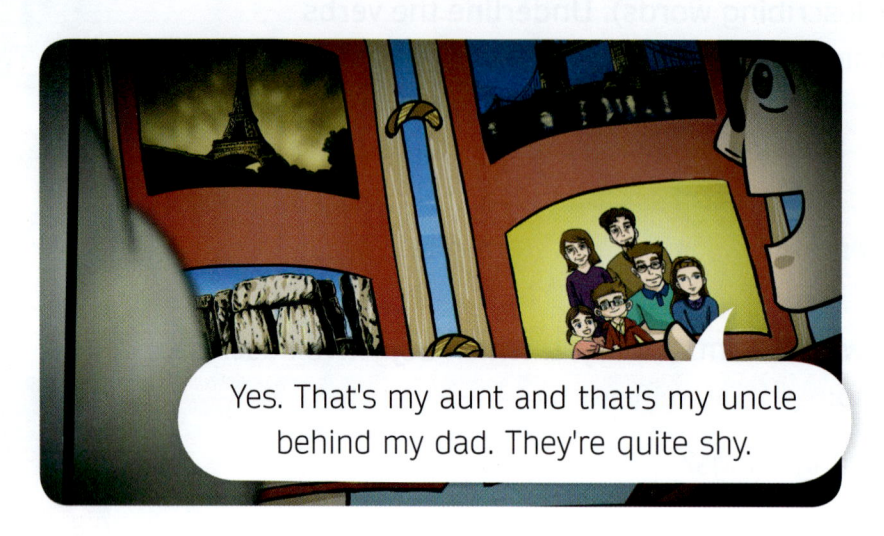

> Yes. That's my aunt and that's my uncle behind my dad. They're quite shy.

1 What did Jack and the Doctor find in the box?
2 What does Jack remember about Stonehenge?

2 Read the grammar box and match.

Grammar

Who **do you look like**?
I **look like** my dad. We both have blond hair.

Who **does he/she look like**?
He/She looks like his/her dad. They both have blue eyes.

Who **are you like**?
I'm like my mom. We're both pretty stubborn.

Who **is he/she like**?
He's/She's like her mom. They're both shy.

1 Who do you like look like?
2 Who does she look like?

a She looks like her sister.
b I look like my dad.

---

3 Read *Nature or Nurture?* again and circle examples of *look like* and *is/are like*. Then read and circle.

1 *Look like* describes people who have similar **physical appearance** / **personality**.
2 *Be like* describes people who have similar **physical appearance** / **personality**.

4 Read, choose, and write. Can you add more examples?

creative   curly hair   forgetful   funny   gray eyes
honest   small mouth   tall

look like	be like

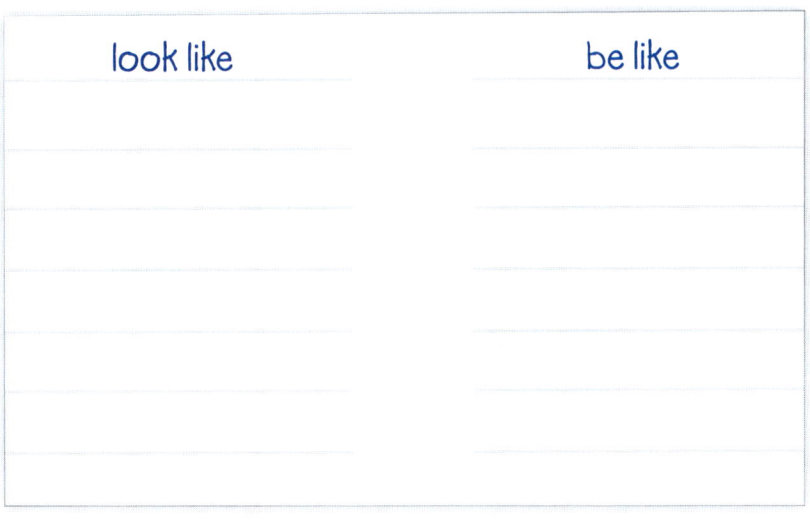

5 Read and complete. Use *look like* or *be like*.

1. My mom .... my aunt. They both have blue eyes and blond hair.
2. I .... my sister – we're both stubborn.
3. My best friend .... her sister. They're tall and slim.
4. Everyone says I .... my dad – we have the same nose and eyes.
5. I think I .... my best friend. We're both honest and open.
6. Natasha .... her sister. They're both forgetful.

Speaking 2

> **Speaking strategy**
>
> Express strong opinions.

6 Think about your family. Who do you look like? Who are you like? Discuss with a friend.

Who do you look like?

I look a lot like my dad. We both have blue eyes and brown hair.

Who are you like?

I'm exactly like my grandma. We're both forgetful.

177

Writing

1 Scan the text. Answer the questions.

1 Who does Esme describe?
2 How are the girls similar?
3 What do they have in common?

2 Read the text. Check your answers from Activity 1.

Me and My Best Friend

I'm Esme and I'm 11 years old. My best friend, Monica, is 11, too. I think we're good friends because we're pretty similar. I think we're like each other in character, too – we're both talkative, creative, and a bit stubborn. Monica is really honest and thoughtful, she always thinks of my feelings and I just love her company. Sometimes we argue but not often! We also have a lot in common – we both like to do sports and we like the same music. We look like each other – we both have long, dark hair and brown eyes.

3 Read the text again and think about the adjectives used. Then compare yourself and a friend and complete the chart.

Similar in character	Interests in common	Similar in physical appearance

4 Find or draw a picture of a friend to describe. Then go to the Workbook to do the writing activity.

Writing strategy

When you write a descriptive text, use a variety of adjectives to add depth to your description.

Now I Know

1 How are we similar but different? Look back through Unit 11. Use the information you learned to answer the questions. Add your own ideas.

1 What makes a good friend?

....

2 Is it important to have something in common with your friends?

....

3 Think about your family and friends. Who do you look like? Who are you like?

....

2 Choose a project.

Do a friendship class survey.

1 Work in pairs or small groups.
2 Make a list of qualities you think are important in a friend.
3 Do a class survey. Which quality is the most important?
4 Record the results in a tally chart.
5 Present your findings to the class.

or

Research your family.

1 Find pictures of your family. Do your family members look similar?
2 Find out what your grandparents and great-grandparents look/looked like and are/were like.
3 Who are you most like?
4 Present your findings to the class.

Read and circle for yourself.

I can identify opinions. I can understand details in extended dialogs.

I can talk about personal experiences. I can describe similarities between appearances.

I can identify supporting details. I can draw simple conclusions.

I can describe similarities between two people.

12

How did people live in the past?

Listening
- I can understand details in extended dialogs.

Reading
- I can get the gist of short texts.
- I can infer about characters' motives.

Speaking
- I can talk about past experiences.
- I can explain the meaning of a word.

Writing
- I can write about personal experiences.

1 💬 Look at the picture and discuss.

1 What can you see in the picture?
2 Did the streets look different 100 years ago? How? Why?

2 Look at the video still in Activity 3 and answer the questions. Then compare your answers with a friend.

1 What can you see in the picture?
2 What do you think school life was like in the past?

3 ▶ 12-1 BBC Watch the video and check your answers from Activity 2. Then watch again and answer the questions.

1 What happened to boys and girls in a Victorian school?
2 How did education differ for girls and boys?
3 What does the teacher ask the boys to repeat?
4 Do you think the lessons in a Victorian school were formal or informal?

181

Pre-reading 1

1 💬 Discuss with a friend.

1 What important inventions can you think of?
2 How have they changed our lives?
3 Do you know when they were invented?

> **Reading strategy**
>
> Compare different experiences to describe the impact of a historical event.

2 💡 Read and match each newspaper headline to a nineteenth-century invention. What do you know about each one?

1
May 29, 1879
Electric Light!

2
March 7, 1876
Going Underground!

3
August 2, 1826
A View from the Window

a The first subway train journey was made in London.
b Thomas Edison invented the first light bulb.
c The first picture was taken in France.

3 🎧 3-16 Read *Railway Revolution!*. What nineteenth-century invention is it about?

Reading 1

September 27, 1826

The Daily News

Railway Revolution!

One year ago, on September 27, 1825, we reported on the first, historic journey of Locomotion No. 1. This famous steam engine was designed and built by the engineer George Stephenson and became the first passenger locomotive in the world. On that historic day, George Stephenson himself drove Locomotion No. 1, carrying 600 passengers on a thrilling ride at speeds of up to 24 kilometers per hour. Thousands of people came to **marvel** at the sight and to cheer the **locomotive** on. It was a proud moment for the whole country.

In today's newspaper, we talk to some ordinary people about the impact of the **railway** on their everyday lives.

> " We used to travel from our small village to the closest town by **horse and cart** to buy food. It was a long, hard journey. But now we can get to town quickly on the train. We can buy fresh bread from the **baker** and meat from the **butcher**. It's marvelous. "
> ☞ *John Smith*

> " The locomotive is wonderful. We can take the children to the seaside on the weekend. They didn't use to know what the ocean was, but now they love having fun at the beach. The train brings fresh fish from the coast every day, too, so we can eat better.
> ☞ *Bertha Smith*

> "We used to live in a tiny cottage next to the factory, but the air was very polluted. Now, thanks to the train, we can live outside the town in one of the new **suburbs** – the houses are bigger and it's nice and quiet. I take the train to the factory every day to work, but I can live somewhere more pleasant."
> ☞ *Frederick Green*

> "I used to work on my family's farm in the country. It was hard work, and I didn't use to get paid much. But now, thanks to Mr. Stephenson's locomotive train I can travel to the city to work in the factory. They call it **commuting**. I earn more money now, and the work isn't as hard. I hear that they're building a tunnel under the Thames in London, and that one day there might be something called a **subway** with trains underground. That would be incredible!"
> ☞ *Benjamin Giles*

> "Well, the railway is right at the bottom of my farm, close to where my cows and sheep graze. It used to be nice and quiet here. Now the noise of the train is terrible, and it terrifies my animals. And the smoke from the train is dirty and pollutes my fields."
> ☞ *Farmer Jones*

> "My **sons** used to live with us and help on the farm. But now they travel by train to the **cotton mills** in town to work. They think the train is fast and exciting, but I just find it noisy and dirty. I feel lonely now; it's just me and my husband left to take care of the farm."
> ☞ *Mrs. Jones*

4 Whose point of view do you most agree with? Why?

Comprehension 1

1 Read *Railway Revolution!* again and answer.

1 What's the newspaper report about?
2 Do you think people liked the trains?

2 Read and write **T** (true) or **F** (false).

1 *Locomotion No. 1* was the first passenger train in the world. ....
2 George Stephenson was a train driver. ....
3 A lot of people came to see the train's first journey. ....
4 The train traveled faster than any transport before. ....
5 The train helped people get to work quickly. ....
6 Everybody liked the new train. ....

3 Find and write four positives and four negatives about the new train.

Positives	Negatives

4 Imagine you're a passenger on the first journey of *Locomotion No. 1*. Can you describe how you feel? What do you see/smell/hear on the journey? Discuss with a friend.

Listening 1

5 What do we use electricity for? How would our lives be different without electricity?

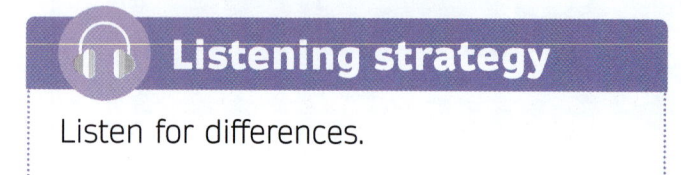

> **Listening strategy**
> Listen for differences.

6 🎧 3-17 Listen to the conversation. Who's talking? What are they talking about?

7 🎧 3-18 Listen again. Check (✓) the things people used to do before they had electricity at home.

watch TV ☐ use candles ☐
go to bed early ☐ surf the internet ☐
write letters ☐ talk to each other ☐
do jigsaw puzzles ☐ read e-books ☐

8 Which electrical machine would it be hardest to live without? Why? Discuss with a friend.

Vocabulary 1

1 Find these words in *Railway Revolution!*. What do you think they mean?

> baker   butcher
> commute   cotton mill
> horse and cart
> locomotive   marvel
> railway   suburb   subway

2 🎧 3-19 Listen and say. Use the words from Activity 1.

3 Complete with the words from Activity 1. Can you think of more words to add?

| Transportation and travel |

| Places in town |

| Places to live |

4 Read and complete the text. Use the words from Activity 1.

Life in the past was very different to life today. A lot of people lived in small villages and worked on farms in the country. They had to use candles for light because they didn't have electricity. They didn't have cars, so they traveled by ¹_____. The coming of the ²_____ changed the way people traveled. People could travel more easily to the cities to work in factories and ³_____. Nowadays, a lot of people live in ⁴_____ outside the city and ⁵_____ by bus, train, or ⁶_____.

5 💬 Discuss with a friend.

1. Would you prefer to live in a city or a village? Why?
2. Would you like to work in a factory or cotton mill? Why?/Why not?
3. Do your parents have to commute to work?

Grammar 1

1 🎬 12-2 [BBC] **Watch Part 1 of the story video. Answer the questions. Then read and complete.**

Look at the trams and .... workers.
Look at the factory! No big .... here.

They used to travel to work by bike.
They didn't use to have supermarkets.

1. What century is it?
2. Where did the factory workers live?
3. How long did it take them to travel to work?
4. Why were they weak?

2 Read the grammar box and complete.

3 Read *Railway Revolution!* again and circle examples of *used to* and *didn't use to*. Then check (✓).

Used to describes

a repeated action over a period of time in the past. ☐

an action that happened once in the past. ☐

Grammar

I/You/She/They **used to** work in the factory.
I/You/He/We **didn't use to** work on the farm.
Did you/she/they **use to** work in the factory?

Yes, I/you/he/they **did**.
No, I/you/she/we **didn't**.

1. Did they use to travel by subway?
   No, ...
2. Did they use to work hard?
   Yes, ...

186

4 Read and complete. Use *used to* or *use to*.

Billy: Mom, did you ¹ _____ play video games when you were young?

Mom: No, we didn't have video games then. And we didn't have smartphones!

Billy: What did you ² _____ play with then?

Mom: We ³ _____ play with other toys. I ⁴ _____ play with my dolls. My friends and I ⁵ _____ make up stories and role-play them.

Billy: Didn't you ⁶ _____ get bored?

Mom: No, I didn't ⁷ _____ get bored! We had a lot of fun then, even without smartphones and computers!

5 Check (✓) the sentences that are correct.

1. My grandma used to go swimming every day when she was young. ☐
2. We used to go on vacation to Spain last week. ☐
3. In the nineteenth century, people didn't use to watch TV. ☐
4. My mom used to wear a nice dress to the party last night. ☐
5. Did you use to go to the movies yesterday? ☐
6. Did you use to suck your thumb when you were a baby? ☐

Speaking 1

6 💬 Imagine your grandparents when they were young. What did they use to do? Discuss with a friend.

> **Speaking strategy**
> Ask questions to find out more.

What did your grandparents used to play with when they were young?

My grandma used to play with her dolls. She didn't use to play video games.

Pre-reading 2

1 What do you think children's lives were like in the past? Discuss with a friend.

> **Reading strategy**
>
> Describe the motivation of characters in a story.

2 Read and answer. Who's telling the story? Where does he work? Do you think he likes his job?

> My name is Albert Smith. I'm eight years old. I live in one small room with my father and my brothers and sisters. Our mother died last year and my father is ill and can't work. So, me and my brothers and sisters have to go out to work to earn money. My sisters work on the street as flower sellers and my brothers work in the coal mine. I work in the cotton mill – I have small fingers that are good for making thread. It's hard work, but someone has to do it.

3 🎧 3-20 Read *William's Lucky Day*. Find out what happens to William.

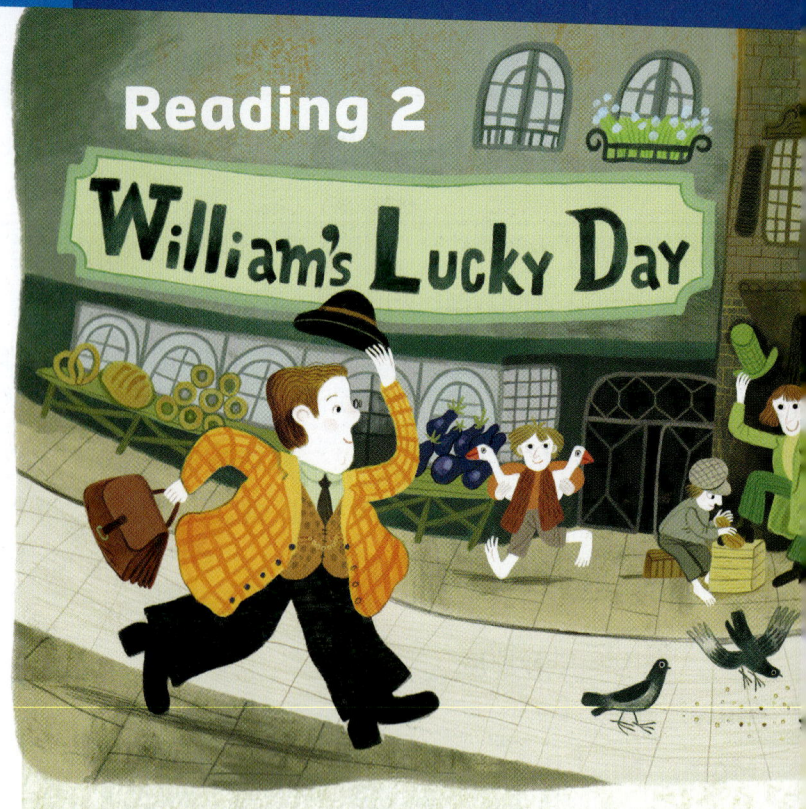

Reading 2

William's Lucky Day

It was time for me to go to the hospital where I worked as a doctor. I put on my coat and hat, put my wallet in my back pocket, and stepped outside. The street was noisy and full of people. The factory workers were on their way to work. Some of them were children, as young as eight or nine years old – their small fingers did jobs that big adult fingers couldn't do, and they cleaned under the machines where adults couldn't reach.

It was a hard life for them, although it was better than working deep underground in the **coal mines**. Many of the children who worked in dark and dangerous conditions ended up in the hospital with terrible injuries.

Meanwhile, on the street young boys were **running errands** – taking fresh bread to the big houses where the rich people lived, or delivering newspapers. The **ratcatchers** were out, chasing the rats that spread disease all around the city. The **flower girls** were on the street selling their ribbons, matches and flowers.

I stopped to buy some matches and then waited to cross the road. A **street sweeper**, a boy of about 10, cleared the horse dung from the road so that I could cross. I gave him a penny, but before I could cross I heard shouting behind me. I looked around to see a police officer holding a young boy, aged about six.

He was tiny and dressed in old, dirty clothes. He had no shoes, and his face was covered with black **soot**.

"Let me go!" he shouted. "I need to get to work!"
"Where do you work, boy?" shouted the police officer.

"I work as a **chimney sweep**. I clean the chimneys at the big house. If I don't go to work, I'll be sent to the **workhouse**!" shouted the boy.

The workhouse was the place where poor people were sent when they had no jobs. It was a horrible place, so I could understand why the boy was terrified of going there.

"Empty your pockets!" shouted the police officer. Slowly, the boy emptied his pockets. A large wallet fell out onto the ground. The police officer picked it up and took out the money inside. "You're a thief – a **pickpocket**!" he shouted. "Where's your mother?"

"My mother's at home, Sir! She used to be a **housemaid**. She worked for the lady in the big house, washing and cleaning. But now she's ill, so she can't work, and father's dead. I sweep chimneys to get some money to help her. Please, Sir, don't send me to the workhouse … or to prison!"

At that moment I felt my back pocket. I realised that my wallet was missing! As I approached the police officer to report the crime, the poor boy looked up at me. He looked so terrified that I started to feel sorry for him. It was a hard life for these poor children and as a doctor, I wanted to help.

"Sir," I said to the police officer. "I'm a doctor. This boy works for me. He sweeps my chimney and runs errands. I gave him my wallet to look after. I'll take it now, thank you!"

The boy and the police officer looked at me in astonishment. The police officer returned my wallet and had no choice but to let the boy go.

The boy smiled gratefully and raced off up the street. It wasn't often that rich people were kind to him. It was his lucky day!

4 Why do you think children had to work in the past?

Comprehension 2

1 Read *William's Lucky Day* again and answer.

1 Who's telling the story?
2 What happens to him?
3 Do you think the street in the story would be different now?

2 Read and circle.

1 Children worked in factories because they **enjoyed the work / could do jobs that adults couldn't**.
2 Working in a coal mine was **dangerous / better than working in a factory**.
3 In the past, a lot of children used to work **in offices / on the street**.
4 The boy who stole the wallet was **poor and hard-working / rich and lazy**.

3 Read and write.

1 Name three jobs children used to do.

2 Describe the pickpocket.

3 Why do you think the boy stole the doctor's wallet?

4 How do you think the doctor felt about the jobs children had to do?

5 How did the doctor help the boy?

4 Do you think children's lives are better now than in the past? Why? Discuss with a friend.

Listening 2

Listening strategy
Listen for similarities.

5 🎧 3-21 Listen to the talk. Where is it? What is it about?

6 🎧 3-22 Listen again and match.

kaleidoscope   zoetrope

1	Children played soccer with a ball	a showed moving pictures.
2	Girls used to play	b toy soldiers and trains.
3	Rich boys used to play with	c a rocking horse.
4	A zoetrope was a toy that	d with dolls and jump ropes.
5	A kaleidoscope was a tube that	e that was made of animal skin.
6	A wooden horse that moved was called	f you looked through to see colorful designs.

7 Which toys from the past do we still have today? How are toys different now? Discuss with a friend.

Vocabulary 2

1 Find these words in *William's Lucky Day*. Which words are jobs that children used to do?

> chimney sweep   coal mine
> flower girl   housemaid
> pickpocket   ratcatcher
> run errands   soot
> street sweeper   workhouse

2 Read and circle.

I'm Fred. I'm 10 years old. I used to be a ¹ **chimney sweep / street sweeper**, but now I'm too big to fit up the chimneys, so I have to do something else. I tried being a ² **pickpocket / flower girl**, but I got caught by the police and I had to go to prison for a week. Now I do two jobs. I sometimes ³ **run / make** errands for rich people. And I also work as a ⁴ **housemaid / ratcatcher**. I like it because I get money for each animal that I catch. And it's better than working underground in a ⁵ **coal mine / workhouse** and getting covered in ⁶ **dung / soot**.

3 Write the job title for each advertisement.

1. **Are you very small?** Do you like climbing chimneys and getting covered in soot? If so, this is the perfect job for you.
   ....

2. **DO YOU WANT TO WORK WITH ANIMALS?** Can you run fast? This could be the job for you!
   ....

3. Are you good at cleaning? Do you like washing clothes and ironing? If so, you'll love this job.
   ....

4. Do you like working outside? Are you good at sweeping? Do you like the smell of horses?
   ....

4 💬 Discuss with a friend.

1. Do you ever run errands? What do you do?
2. Which of the jobs from the past would you choose to do? Why?

> I sometimes run errands for my mom. I go to the corner store to buy bread and milk.

> I would like to be a flower girl because I like flowers.

Grammar 2

1 Watch Parts 2 and 3 of the story video. Then answer the questions.

Let's defeat the Smogator. The alien .... tried to take over the Earth!

The Doctor is the man who defeated the Smogator.

1 How did the Doctor and Kim make the workers go home?
2 What did they use to defeat the Smogator?
3 Who do you think built the Super Slim Battery?

2 Read the grammar box and match.

Grammar

This is the machine **that** makes the pollution.
Doctor Who is the man **who** defeated the Smogator.
The village is the place **where** the workers lived.

1 The factory was the place
2 The Super Slim Battery was the thing
3 Jack Green is the scientist

a that helped defeat the Smogator.
b who made the Super Slim Battery.
c where Doctor Who found the Smogator.

3 Read *William's Lucky Day* again. Circle examples of relative clauses with *that*, *who*, and *where*. Then complete.

.... defines an object   .... defines a person   .... defines a place

192

4 Read and complete. Use *that*, *who*, or *where*.

1 George Stephenson was the man .... built the world's first locomotive.
2 The light bulb was an invention .... changed people's lives.
3 A factory is a place .... people work.
4 The internet is a network .... connects computers across the world.
5 A governess was someone .... used to teach children at home.
6 A school is a place .... children learn.

5 Write sentences about these things, people, and places. Use *that*, *who*, or *where*.

1 Tim Berners Lee / man / invent internet
Tim Berners Lee is the man who invented the internet.

2 television / machine / shows moving pictures
....

3 London / city / see Big Ben
....

4 Big Ben / big clock / tells time
....

5 Neymar Jr. / soccer player / Brazil
....

6 Shakira / singer / Colombia
....

7 Chichén Itzá / city / see Mayan ruins
....

Speaking 2

6 Work with a friend. Can you define these things, people, or places? Use *that*, *who*, or *where*.

Acapulco beach
Buckingham Palace
computer   **Istanbul**
Lionel Messi   **Mexico City**
telephone   **newspaper**

Buckingham Palace is the place where the Queen of England lives.

The telephone is a machine that helps people talk to each other.

Writing

1 Scan the text. Answer the questions.

1. How did the girl travel?
2. Where did she go?
3. How did she feel about her journey?

2 Read the text. Check your answers from Activity 1.

A Day at the Seaside!

Today I traveled on a locomotive train for the first time! I went on a day trip to the seaside with my family. I saw the ocean and the beach for the first time in my life! The smell of the ocean is something I will remember forever. The noise of the train was so loud but it was so exciting! And I could smell the smoke. The fields and country flashed by very quickly. It was fantastic and I felt very excited! Before, we used to travel very slowly by horse and cart. Now we can travel easily and quickly to new places. I think the railway will make communication so much easier and faster. I really hope my family and I can return to the ocean soon. I felt so happy there.

July 12, 1835

3 Read the text again and look at the way the author has applied the strategy. Circle the thoughts and feelings the author shares.

4 **WB 169** Find or draw pictures of how the railway changed the lives of children in the nineteenth century. Then go to the Workbook to do the writing activity.

Writing strategy

Write descriptions of thoughts and feelings to show the response of a character to a situation.

When he went in the coal mine, he felt very scared.

Now I Know

1 How did people live in the past? Look back through Unit 12. Use the information you've learned to answer the questions.

1 How did people use to travel/work/play in the past?

....

2 How's life different now?

....

3 What do you think are the three most important inventions of the last century? Why?

....

2 Choose a project.

Make a poster about children's lives in the past.

1. Choose one of these subjects – school life, work, or toys. Work in pairs or small groups.
2. Find out as much as you can.
3. Make a poster with pictures and present your findings to the class.

or

Research an invention that changed people's lives.

1. Decide on an invention.
2. Find information about the invention: Who invented it? When? How did it change people's lives?
3. Write about the invention. Add illustrations where appropriate and present to the class.

Read and circle for yourself.

I can understand details in extended dialogs.

I can talk about past experiences. I can explain the meaning of a word.

I can get the gist of short texts. I can infer about characters' motives.

I can write about of personal experiences.

195

Dictionary

Unit 1
Key vocabulary

beef *noun* meat from a cow
boiled *adj.* food cooked in very hot water
bread roll *noun* a small round piece of bread
broccoli *noun* a vegetable with green stems and green or purple flowers
butter *noun* a fatty spread made by churning cream
calcium *noun* a silver-white metal that helps to form strong teeth and bones
carbohydrate *noun* a substance in foods such as sugar that gives your body energy
dairy *noun* foods made from milk, such as butter, cheese, and yogurt
fat *noun* an oily substance in food such as milk, cheese, or butter
fiber *noun* the parts of plants that you eat but cannot digest, which help food to move through your body
fried *adj.* cooked in hot oil
grilled *adj.* food cooked on a frame over a fire
iron *noun* a natural substance that is in food and your blood in small amounts
jelly *noun* a sweet food made with fruit juice that is solid but shakes when you move it
mineral *noun* a substance that is formed naturally in the earth, such as coal, salt, stone, or gold
miso *soup noun* a Japanese soup thickened with miso paste
noodle *noun* a long thin piece of food made from a mixture of flour, water, and eggs, usually cooked in soup or boiling water
oil *noun* a plant, animal, or synthetic fat used for cooking with
omelet *noun* eggs mixed together and cooked in a pan without stirring. You usually put cheese or vegetables in an omelet and then fold it over
pancake *noun* a thin, flat food made from flour, milk, and eggs that is cooked in a pan and eaten hot
protein *noun* a substance in food such as meat or eggs that helps your body to grow
salmon *noun* a large fish with silver skin and pink flesh
vegetable *noun* a plant you can eat, such as a carrot or a cabbage
vitamin *noun* a chemical substance found in food that is necessary for good health

Unit 2
Key vocabulary

arches *noun* structures with curved tops that support the weight of a bridge or building
architect *noun* someone who designs buildings
attract *verb* if a place or thing attracts people or animals, they go to it because it is interesting or good

belfry *noun* a tower for a bell, especially on a church
bridge *noun* a structure built over a river or road
brochures *noun* thin books that give information or advertises something
camp *noun* a place where children stay and do activities during their vacation
carved *adj.* a piece of wood or stone cut into a shape
concrete *noun* a substance used for building that is made by mixing sand, water, small stones, and cement
construction *noun* the process of building something such as a house, bridge, or road
landmark *noun* something that helps you recognize where you are, such as a famous building
massive *adj.* very big
medieval *adj.* relating to the time between the 5th and 15th centuries A.D.
meter *noun* a unit of length measuring 100 centimeters or approximately 39.37 inches
modern *adj.* belonging to the present time or most recent time
monastery *noun* a place where monks live
monument *noun* something that is built so that people will remember an important event or person
mural *noun* a large painting on a wall
package *noun* something that has been packed in a box or wrapped in paper, and then sent by mail or delivered
staircase *noun* a set of stairs inside a building
statue *noun* a model of a person or animal made from metal or stone
structure *noun* something that has been built
tower *noun* a tall narrow building or part of a building
typical *adj.* having the usual qualities of a particular person, group, or thing

Unit 3
Key vocabulary

bamboo *noun* a tall tropical plant with hollow stems, often used for making furniture
bluefin tuna *noun* a large fish that lives in the ocean
coral *noun* a hard pink, white, or red substance formed from the bones of very small sea animals
destroy *verb* to end the existence of something by damaging it so badly.
disappear *verb* to cease to exist
endangered *adj.* a type of animal or plant that soon might not exist anymore because there are very few left
glide *verb* to move smoothly and quietly, as if without effort
gorilla *noun* a large strong animal that looks like a monkey
hectare *noun* a unit for measuring an area of land, equal to 10,000 square meters

leatherback turtle *noun* an animal with a thick curved shell that covers its body
national park *noun* an area of countryside or fresh water that is protected by the state
poacher *noun* someone who catches animals illegally
polar bear *noun* a large white bear that lives near the North Pole
predator *noun* an animal that kills and eats other animals
prevent *verb* to stop something from happening, or stop someone from doing something
rainforest *noun* a thick forest in a part of the world that is hot and wet
roam *verb* to walk or travel all over a place
shell *noun* the hard part that protects the body of an animal such as a crab, turtle, or snail
snow leopard *noun* a large wild cat with yellow fur and black spots
species *noun* a group of animals or plants of the same kind
survive *verb* to continue to live after an accident, war, illness, etc
tusk *noun* one of the two long pointed teeth that grow outside the mouth of some animals, such as elephants
whisper *verb* to talk very quietly

Unit 4
Key vocabulary

cans *noun* metal containers that hold food
cardboard *noun* very thick stiff paper
create *verb* to make or bring something into existence
cup *noun* a small round container that you drink from
decoration *noun* a pretty thing that you use to make something look more attractive
fleece *noun* the woolly coat of a sheep
fumes *noun* gas or vapor that smells strongly and is dangerous to breathe
glass jars *noun* glass containers with a lid. You store food in jars
landfill *noun* a site where waste is disposed, usually by filling an excavated pit
metal *noun* a hard substance, such as iron, or steel, that is good at conducting electricity and heat
natural resource *noun* things that exist in nature and can be used by people, for example oil, trees, etc
packaging *noun* the bags, boxes, etc that a product is sold in
picture frame *noun* a structure made of wood or metal, that surrounds a picture
plastic *noun* a synthetic material that can be shaped while soft before it sets
process *verb* to deal with information by putting it through a system or computer
recycling plant *noun* a factory that puts old paper, glass, or other materials through a special process so that they can be used again

soil *noun* the earth in which plants grow
stuff *noun* a variety of things or objects.
throw out *verb* to get rid of something that you do not want or need
tire *noun* a thick round piece of rubber that fits around the wheel of a car or bicycle
toilet paper roll *noun* soft, thin paper that you use to clean yourself after you have used the toilet
toxic fumes *noun* strong-smelling gas or smoke that is poisonous to breath in
upcycle *verb* to change something old in a way that makes it better or more valuable than it was before
wood *noun* the hard material that trees are made of

Unit 5
Key vocabulary

athlete *noun* someone who competes in sports such as running or jumping
barber *noun* a person whose job is to cut men's hair
brush *noun* a thing that you use for cleaning, painting, tidying your hair, etc
comfortable *adj.* something that is comfortable makes you feel physically relaxed
compete *verb* to try to win something or to be more successful than someone else
compose *verb* to write a piece of music
crew *noun* all the people that work together on a ship, plane, etc
delicious *adj.* very pleasant to taste or smell
discover *verb* to find someone or something, either by accident or because you were looking for them
discuss *verb* to talk about something with someone in order to exchange ideas or decide something
explorer *noun* someone who travels to places that people have not visited before
fast *adj.* moving, happening, or doing something quickly
hard *adj.* not soft, and difficult to press down, cut, or break
journey *noun* an occasion when you travel from one place to another, especially over a long distance
lab *noun* a laboratory, a room where scientists work and do experiments
late *adj.* arriving, happening, or done after the time that was expected or arranged
musician *noun* someone who plays a musical instrument, especially as a job
painter *noun* someone who paints pictures
sailor *noun* someone who sails on boats or ships, especially as a job
self-portrait *noun* a picture of yourself, done by you
studio *noun* a room where a painter or photographer works or where music is recorded
surgeon *noun* a doctor who does operations in a hospital
terrifying *adj.* making someone very frightened
train *verb* to prepare for a sports competition by exercising and practicing

Unit 6
Key vocabulary

adapt to *verb* to change because you are in a new situation
ash *noun* the gray powder that is left after something has burned
beat *verb* to make a regular sound or movement
collapse *verb* to fall down suddenly
crater *noun* the round open top of a volcano
dehydrated *adj.* not having enough water in your body
eruption *noun* an occasion when a volcano erupts, sending smoke, fire, and rock into the sky
explosion *noun* when something such as a bomb explodes, and bursts into small pieces with a loud noise and a lot of force
extreme *adj.* very great in amount or severity
heart rate *noun* the number of heart beats per minute
heatstroke *noun* fever and weakness caused by being outside in the heat of the sun for too long
hypothermia *noun* a serious medical condition in which a person's body becomes too cold
in danger *phrase* to be in a situation in which someone or something may be harmed or something bad may happen
lava *noun* hot melted rock that flows from a volcano
medallion *noun* a piece of metal like a large coin, worn on a chain around someone's neck
mild *adj.* mild weather is not too hot and not too cold
numb *adj.* not able to feel anything
perspire *verb* to sweat
safe *adj.* if someone or something is safe, they will not be harmed
shake *verb* to move up and down or from side to side with quick movements, or to make something do this
shiver *verb* if you shiver, your body shakes slightly because you are cold or frightened
sweat *noun* liquid that comes out through your skin when you are hot
tremor *noun* a small earthquake
volcano *noun* a mountain with a large hole at the top, through which lava (=very hot liquid rock) is sometimes forced out

Unit 7
Key vocabulary

artificial fiber *noun* a type of thread that is not natural, but made by people
belt *noun* a band of leather or cloth that you wear around your waist
borrow *verb* to use something that belongs to someone else and give it back to them later
bracelet *noun* a piece of jewelry that you wear around your wrist
cardigan *noun* a knitted sweater that fastens down the front
collar *noun* the part of a shirt, coat, dress, etc that fits around your neck
cotton *noun* cloth or thread made from the cotton plant
delicate *adj.* easily damaged or broken
denim *noun* a hard-wearing cotton twill fabric, typically blue and used for jeans
design *noun* the way that something is planned or made
dress up *verb* to wear special clothes for fun
earring *noun* a piece of jewelry you fasten to your ear
jewelry *noun* small things that you wear for decoration, such as rings and necklaces
leather *noun* animal skin used for making shoes, bags, etc
necklace *noun* a piece of jewelry that you wear around your neck
patterned *adj.* decorated with an arrangement of shapes, lines, and colors
ribbon *noun* a narrow piece of attractive cloth that you use, for example, to tie your hair or hold things together
silk *noun* soft cloth made from the threads produced by a type of caterpillar
suit *noun* a jacket and trousers or a skirt that are made of the same material and are worn together
tights *noun* a piece of women's clothing that fits closely around the feet and legs and up to the waist
vest *noun* a waistcoat or sleeveless jacket
watch *noun* a small clock that you wear on your wrist
wool *noun* the soft thick hair of a sheep, used to make cloth or thread

Unit 8
Key vocabulary

action *noun* a movie with lots of fast exciting scenes
animation *noun* the process of making movies with drawings or models, rather than filming actors
applause *noun* the sound of people hitting their hands together to show that they have enjoyed a play, concert, speaker, etc
audience *noun* the people who watch or listen to a performance
ballet *noun* a type of dancing that tells a story with music but no words, or a performance of this type of dancing
ballroom dancing *noun* a formal type of dancing that is done with a partner and has different steps for different types of music
comedy *noun* a funny movie, play, or television program that makes people laugh
director *noun* the person who tells the actors what to do in a movie or play
drama *noun* a play, television program, or serious movie that tells a story
edit *verb* to make changes to a movie before it is shown to public audiences
hip-hop *noun* a type of modern popular music with a strong beat that people dance to

hiplet™ *noun* a dance that combines the movements of ballet with the movements and music from hip-hop
horror *noun* a movie or story in which strange and frightening things happen
jive *noun* a very fast dance, popular especially in the 1930s and 1940s, performed to fast jazz music
lines *noun* a row of words in a poem, play, song, or book
make-up *noun* colored substances that you put on your face to improve or change your appearance
performance *noun* an occasion when someone entertains people by performing a play or a piece of music
play *noun* a story that actors perform in a theater or on the radio
reality TV *noun* television programs that film ordinary people doing their jobs or living their lives, or show what they do when put in a special situation
rhythm *noun* a regular repeated pattern of sounds or movements
rock *noun* a type of loud modern music, that uses drums and guitars
samba *noun* a fast dance from Brazil, or the type of music played for this dance
tango *noun* a fast dance from South America, or music for this dance
waltz *noun* a fairly slow dance with a regular pattern of three beats

Unit 9
Key vocabulary

battle *verb* to try hard to achieve something or deal with something
challenge *noun* something that tests your skill or ability, especially in a way that is interesting
endurance *noun* the ability to continue doing something difficult or painful
exhaustion *noun* extremely tired
eye patch *noun* a piece of material worn over one eye, usually because that eye has been damaged
history *noun* the things that happened or existed in the past
huge *adj.* extremely large
island *noun* a piece of land surrounded by water
loneliness *noun* unhappy because you are alone or do not have any friends
metal detector *noun* a machine used for finding metal objects
moonlight *noun* the light of the moon
mystery *noun* something that is difficult to explain or understand
navigate *verb* to decide which way a car or ship should go, using maps
nervously *adverb* in a worried manner.
nonstop *adj.* without stopping
point *verb* to direct something in a particular direction.
rope *noun* very strong thick string
scar *noun* a permanent mark on someone's skin from a cut or wound

sink *verb* to go down, or make something go down, below the surface of water
solo *adj.* done alone, without anyone else helping you
sword *noun* a weapon with a long, sharp blade and a handle
treacherous *adj.* dangerous
yachtsman *noun* a man who sails a yacht

Unit 10
Key vocabulary

care for *verb* to do things for someone who is old or sick, or for a young child
charity *noun* an organization that gives money, goods, or help to people who are poor, sick, etc
collect *verb* to get things and bring them together
constant *adj.* happening regularly or all the time
donate *verb* to give something, especially money, to a person or organization that needs help
email *noun* an electronic message sent from one computer to another
frequently *adv.* often
generous *adj.* someone who is generous is kind and enjoys giving people things or helping them
helpful *adj.* willing to help
improve *verb* to become better, or to make something better
jerry can *noun* a type of metal container with flat sides that is used to carry liquids
organization *noun* a group of people, companies, or countries that has formed for a particular purpose
raise money *verb* to collect money to help people
regularly *adv.* often
sponsor *verb* to give money to an event or institution, especially in exchange for the right to advertise
support *verb* to say that you agree with an idea, group, or person and want them to succeed
text message *noun* a written message that you send to someone using a mobile phone
volunteer *verb* to do work without being paid
website *noun* a place on the Internet where you can find information about something, especially a particular organization
well *noun* a deep hole dug in the ground, from which people get water

Unit 11
Key vocabulary

active *adj.* energetic and ready to engage in physical pursuits
arrogant *adj.* behaving in an unpleasant or rude way because you think you are more important than other people
behave *verb* to do or say things in a particular way
character *noun* the qualities that make a person, place, or thing different from any other

determine *verb* to directly affect or control what something will be like or what will happen
disagree *verb* to have a different opinion from someone else
feel *verb* to experience an emotion or sensation
forgetful *adj.* someone who is forgetful often forgets things that they should remember
have something in common *phrase* belonging to or shared by two or more people or things
honest *adj.* someone who is honest does not lie, cheat, or steal
imaginative *adj.* good at thinking of interesting ideas
mean *adj.* cruel and not kind
open *adj.* honest and not hiding anything
positive *adj.* hopeful and confident
practical *adj.* relating to doing things rather than thinking or talking about them
respond *verb* to react to something that has been said or done
similar *adj.* almost the same
stubborn *adj.* refusing to change your mind even when other people criticize you or try to persuade you
talkative *adj.* a talkative person talks a lot
think *verb* to have an opinion about someone or something
thoughtful *adj.* serious and quiet because you are thinking about something
unique *adj.* something that is unique is the only one of its kind
vow *verb* a serious promise

Unit 12

Key vocabulary

baker *noun* someone whose job is making bread, cakes, etc
butcher *noun* someone who owns or works in a shop that sells meat
chimney sweep *noun* someone whose job is to clean the inside of chimneys
coal mine *noun* a place from which coal is dug out of the ground
commute *noun* to regularly travel a long distance to work
cotton mill *noun* a factory where cotton cloth is made
flower girl *noun* a young girl who sells flowers on the street
horse and cart *noun* a vehicle pulled by a horse, used for carrying heavy things or people
housemaid *noun* a female servant who cleans someone's house
locomotive *noun* a train engine
marvel *verb* to look at something with wonder and admiration
pickpocket *noun* someone who steals things from people's pockets or bags in public places

railway *noun* the system of tracks and equipment that trains use
ratcatcher *noun* a person that catches rats
run errands *verb* go somewhere to buy, get, or deliver something
soot *noun* black powder that is produced when something burns
street sweeper *noun* a person who cleans the street
suburb *noun* an area where people live which is on the edge of a city
subway *noun* a railroad that is under the ground in a city
workhouse *noun* a building in Britain in the past where very poor people lived if they had nowhere else to go